What Other Writers Say About
IN SEARCH of FORGIVENESS

This is a brave book—written with passion and extraordinary honesty. Trudi Alexy has written an unforgettable saga that holds the reader in thrall.

—Elizabeth Forsythe Hailey, author of *A Woman Of Independent Means*

In Search of Forgiveness takes us on a journey of hope. In this memoir that could have Nietzsche's words as an epigraph: "That which does not kill us makes us stronger," Alexy demonstrates the glory of the human spirit in overcoming emotional abuse and betrayal, and shows us how she used her experience to birth a new creative professional and personal life.

—Malka Drucker, author of *Holocaust Rescuers*

Both by chance and choice, Trudi Alexy has lived through nearly every cultural and political shift of the last century, from a childhood that began in Prague and Paris and ended with hiding in Fascist Spain during World War II, to the California Watts Riots, Henry Miller's parlor, a tender love affair with a Moroccan diplomat and an audience with King Juan Carlos I of Spain. Opening the door to her heart and her memory with courage, brutal honesty and heartbreaking vulnerability, Alexy looks back on a life of great loss and emotional violence s well as healing, joy and transformation.

A remarkable life, remarkably rendered, this book echoed in my heart long after I put it down.

—Gita Romano, author of *Finding Mia, Finding Me*

In this, the third part of her trilogy, Trudi Alexy burrows ever deeper and deeper into the convoluted lives of Jews forced to conceal their religious identity. Here, beautiful, poised, appearing overly confident, she reveals herself as a victim of suicidal depression. Detailing her shame, mistrust and self-doubt that prompted her to trace her course, she moved from the historic and familial to the inter-personal, and, finally, to herself. Reality and literary skills unfurled, the work is rife with error, heroism, anguish, self-pity, blindness, insight, and, ultimately, acceptance of self and others. It brings to mind other searing memoirs: Memories Of A Catholic Girlhood, Stranger In The City and Angela's Ashes. It makes you want to embrace the author, and even more, to emulate her daring.

—Harriet Rochlin, author of *Pioneer Jews*

Trudi Alexy's In Search of Forgiveness: The Healing Journey to Self-Acceptance is a frank revelation of a complex life troubled by the psychic acid and deep moral dilemma of a Holocaust survivor racked by guilt of having survived by fraud: her Jewish family flees from Prague to Paris after the annexation of Austria in 1938, then to Barcelona where they disguise themselves as Catholics in order to survive, much in the way the medieval Marrano Jews escaped the Spanish Inquisition. Her life becomes an intense search for forgiveness with a myriad of emotional traps throughout the journey—an overpowering mother who prevents her marriage to her true love, an unethical therapist who entangles her in an abusive affair, suicide attempts and divorce. The riveting story of her struggles with depression, her reconciliation with her dying mother, her reconnecting to her true love and her extraction of justice from her therapist—all this creates a breathtaking memoir of a woman's spiritual odyssey. Alexy is a masterful conjurer of place and person-

ality—Andalusia, Barcelona, the literary world of Los Angeles, King Juan Carlos of Spain—something one would expect in fiction more than in this extraordinary memoir.

—Sally Patterson Tubach, Ph.D.

Co-author: *An Uncommon Friendship: From Opposite sides of the Holocaust*
Author: *Memoirs of a Terrorist*

In Search of Forgiveness

In Search of Forgiveness

◆

The Hard but Healing Journey to Self-Acceptance

Trudi Alexy

iUniverse, Inc.
New York Lincoln Shanghai

In Search of Forgiveness
The Hard but Healing Journey to Self-Acceptance

iUniverse books may be ordered through booksellers or by contacting:

iUniverse
2021 Pine Lake Road, Suite 100
Lincoln, NE 68512
www.iuniverse.com
1-800-Authors (1-800-288-4677)

Although the events recorded in this book are factual, the names of some individuals and their locations have been changed to protect their privacy.

ISBN-13: 978-0-595-36054-3 (pbk)
ISBN-13: 978-0-595-81142-7 (cloth)
ISBN-13: 978-0-595-80505-1 (ebk)
ISBN-10: 0-595-36054-8 (pbk)
ISBN-10: 0-595-81142-6 (cloth)
ISBN-10: 0-595-80505-1 (ebk)

Printed in the United States of America

This book is dedicated to all those
who struggle to forgive and accept themselves.

Contents

AUTHOR BIO

Lycée Français de Barcelone
>   1939-1941

Marycliff Academy, Arlington Heights. MA
>   1941-1944

Manhattanville College of the Sacred Heart, New York City, NY
>   1944-49

Jewelry, Fashion Designer
>   New York, San Francisco, Denver, Los Angeles
>   1946-1975

Antioch University, West, Los Angeles, CA
>   Bachelor and Masters Degree in Psychology
>   1976-1979

License in Marriage, Child and Family Counseling
>   Los Angeles, CA,
>   1980

Private Practice, Specialty in Art Therapy
>   1980-2005

Author, Lecturer,
>   1988-present

PROLOGUE

Los Angeles, 2005

Some secrets, if kept hidden too long, turn into psychic acid: they corrode the soul. They force you to question reality, your own as well as others'. Doubt and denial cast a shadow on every experience. Since my early teens I believed I was cursed, certain that I was not entitled to be happy, loved, successful. I had broken a sacred vow that was meant to atone for what I believed was an unforgivable moral transgression, leaving me doubly damned. For years I mistrusted anything good that ever happened to me, and no matter what it was, it either felt unreal, or soon disappeared from my memory.

Most of those around me never guessed the truth. I seemed to lead a charmed life: blessed with a highly regarded husband, two bright children, an impressive and varied career, first as a jewelry and fashion designer and later as a licensed art and family therapist, with support from well-known mentors who believed in me and were there for me in meaningful ways whenever they felt I needed encouragement. Few guessed that I had for years been operating on automatic pilot, like a robot programmed to perform all tasks expected of me. But I derived no emotional satisfaction from praise, felt no joy in recognition, no pride in accomplishment. I felt abandoned by God, and knew that, in the end, any dreams I might allow myself to reach for would prove to be no more than seductive mirages.

Along the way, in despair over ever finding my way back into God's grace, I surrendered my search for forgiveness to a man who betrayed my trust and led me into a moral swamp that threatened to destroy me—until I grew strong enough to break out of my bondage. Despite it all, the memory web that kept weaving and reweaving itself around the first man I ever loved and myself remained stubbornly intact. Nico and I fell in love when both of us were teen-agers and planned to marry. Then World War II separated us. During the years we were apart, after both of us married others and eventually lost our mates, I dared to occasionally imagine a time when Nico and I would live together. But that dream never came true, and now it never will: Nico died two weeks ago. The final chapter of the dark fate I had brought upon myself years ago seemed to have fulfilled itself at last.

1

But, browsing recently through a box of faded photographs, letters, and poems—recapturing fragments of the times Nico and I spent together after years of separation and then finding each other again as older, seasoned veterans of life—I marveled at the miracle that kept our love alive for six decades. Again and again I asked myself: could our love be a sign that I was finally forgiven, that my curse had been lifted, that my life sentence was commuted to time served?

To find the truth, I felt compelled to reach into that most personal hidden part of my past, to uncover answers to questions that had taken me decades to confront.

I had survived by carefully choosing to focus on those parts of my life with which I had somehow managed to come to terms, leaving others buried, certain that reviewing them would bring on only more shame and regret. Most importantly, I remained convinced that examining my past would stir up and intensify the punitive fate that had stalked me since my early teens.

Despite my fear, Nico's death caused my interior floodgates to release a rush of long forgotten events, images of once familiar places, but most especially, a cascade of long repressed feelings. To keep them from disappearing again, I knew I had to look at and re-live them if they were to ever make sense and reveal the reason for their impact on my life. It eventually became clear to me that I had not merely been a spectator but also a passionate participant in one of the most turbulent, earthshaking periods of history: the last seventy-five years of the twentieth century.

There is no way I could retrieve these banished years in any reasonable order because they arose from my subconscious as a maddeningly mixed-up jumble of fact-fragments and feelings, each highlighting and clarifying another facet of my life. So, now, despite my initial resistance to undertaking what at first seemed to be such a risky, highly charged exploration, I am convinced that these buried pockets of my past must not only be torn open, but also shared—if for no other reason than to give hope to anyone who feels, as I did, that some moral transgressions can never be forgiven, and finds that a life that initially appeared to be cursed can be healed and transformed.

1

RETURN to SPAIN

I was thirteen years old in 1941 when my family suddenly announced we would leave Barcelona, where we had lived since fleeing Paris in September 1939, and sail for America. I was devastated. I begged my parents to stay, but during our two years in Spain, they never stopped worrying that the Fascist authorities would discover we were Jewish refugees, and not Catholics, as we claimed, and turn us over to the Nazis who had helped dictator Francisco Franco win the recent civil war. For three years, Hitler and Mussolini had used Spain as a proving ground to test the new mass murder weapons that they later used to devastate Europe during World War II. Much of Spain was in ruins when we sought shelter there, food was scarce, but the Catalán (northeastern Spaniards) people protected us, and kept us safe until we finally obtained the necessary documents to leave for New York.

I loved everything about my life in Spain: sharing Señora Carron's lovely apartment with her housekeeper, Pilar, who took me to church with her every Sunday; my school, the Barcelona Lycée Français; the guitar music echoing through the narrow cobble-stoned streets; the colorful religious processions on holy days and Gaudí's nearby *Pedrera* (stone quarry) apartment building, whose rooftop, with its heraldic chimney pots, had been my private fantasy playground. I was determined to return to Spain as soon as possible.

Now, twenty-three years later, I was finally going back.

My favorite uncle, Milos, visiting Los Angeles after a long absence, became concerned when he found me deeply depressed. I kept evading his questions. How could I confess that I felt desperate, hopeless, that I was ready to do whatever it took to get as far away as possible from home? I could never adequately explain why I just wanted to get lost, to forget everything, to escape from the bondage that paralyzed me.

"What can I do to help?" he asked.

I flashed back to the last time Milos had helped my family. As he would do for thirty-five other Jews who were in danger of being caught by Hitler's hordes and ending up in concentration camps, he used his political connections and friendship with Bernard Baruch to bargain for American entrance visas. He also agreed to the Immigration Department's requirement that he make a substantial financial commitment, guaranteeing to keep all the beneficiaries of his intervention off government assistance rolls until they obtained their working permits and American citizenship papers. In our case, Milos even paid our travel expenses from Barcelona to New York. His generosity ended up costing him far more than he anticipated.

Papa had been a successful entrepreneur in Prague, where we had lived before fleeing to Paris right after the *Anschluss* in 1938. He had uncanny instincts that helped him to know exactly when to get us first out of Prague, and later from Paris, just before Hitler's forces began their sweep across Europe.

But by the time we left Barcelona three years later, Papa was a bitter, broken man, deprived of his real name, his identity, his prestige, his magical foresight no longer in demand—a refugee who could neither use his education nor his experience to establish himself at the level to which he was accustomed and felt entitled—even unable to speak the language of the land.

What made it all the more difficult was that Milos, Papa's younger brother, was well established in the United States since he emigrated from their home in Romania in his teens. He had married into high society by the time he became CEO of a large corporation and was by then a millionaire. Our family's dependence on Milos' help humiliated my once proud Papa. His groundless suspicion that Mama was in love with Milos and involved in a secret affair with him pushed him into paranoia. A month after Papa accepted a position as a technician in the printing plant of the *New York Times*, which Milos had arranged for him, he went to the FBI and denounced Milos as a spy. Although there was no truth to the accusation, the investigation, involving embarrassing interrogations of all his friends and associates, created a scandal. It took Milos six months to clear his name.

Now here he was, offering his help to a family member once again.

"I want to move back to Spain," I blurted out. "It's the only place I was ever happy."

My children, husband…Martin…especially Martin…nothing and no one mattered. I was ready to leave everything, everybody, to get as far away from Los Angeles as possible.

"It's been years since you were there last. Things, places change," Milos warned me. "You might feel differently now."

I burst into tears. "You don't understand! I must get away!"

"Why don't you go for a visit first?" he asked and quickly added, "Would fifteen hundred dollars help?"

The very thought of escaping my situation had an instantly positive effect on my mood. My husband had long watched helplessly as my depression grew worse, so when I told him that Uncle Milos was treating me to a trip to Spain, he was relieved and encouraged me to go. In 1964, fifteen hundred dollars was a small fortune in still touristically under-discovered Spain. Nevertheless, I planned to be careful with my money by hitching rides with people I hoped to meet along the way or traveling by train from city to city, staying in small hostels, and eating inexpensive meals, so that I could stretch Uncle Milos' gift as long as possible. I intended to make it to most of the places I had long wanted to visit, starting in Spain's southern region of Andalusia, where I knew the Moorish influence (with which I had long ago fallen in love while I lived in Barcelona) was most prominent. I dreamed of steeping myself in its mysterious atmosphere, its ancient gardens and exquisite architecture, in Málaga, Granada, Sevilla, Córdoba, and then travel north to Toledo and on to Madrid, ending up in Barcelona, the place to which I had vowed to return nearly a quarter-century ago. I longed to mingle with strangers, forget my life at home, feel free and new, even if only for a few weeks.

Before I left, Martin asked me to leave an approximate itinerary with him, just in case he needed to get in touch with me. I hesitated, but finally told him what cities I thought I might want to visit, although I had no idea if, when or how long I might be there. That way it would be difficult for him to reach me.

"Just check with American Express wherever you are...," he suggested.

I decided to sail rather than fly to Spain to give myself time to get accustomed to the idea of being free, on my own, without needing to hide or justify anything to anyone, following only my long ignored inner compass. By the time the S.S. Saturnia dropped anchor in Málaga, I had left my old self behind.

As soon as I set foot on Spanish soil, I was filled with the same magical feeling I had felt the first time my family and I walked across the French/Spanish border in Port Bou, high in the Pyrenees: a mysterious sense of having come home to a place where I had lived before. I could not explain that feeling then. After all, at that time I knew nothing about Spain or its history: the Golden Age when Jews collaborated with Christians and Moslems to bring Spain to the world's cultural pinnacle, followed by the Inquisition's horrendous persecution of Jews that led to

Spain's final solution—the expulsion of all un-baptized Jews in 1492. Had I known all this, I probably would have been afraid. What was Papa thinking, making us go to a place with such an anti-Semitic past?

There was no way for me to anticipate Spain's impact on my life when I first arrived there as a child of eleven. But by the time I returned in 1964, I had my own experience living there as a point of reference. I was just grateful to experience that familiar, warm feeling again.

I was shocked to find a letter from Martin waiting for me at the American Express office in every city I visited! I realized he must have written each one well before I left, to make sure I would find it on my arrival. In every letter he described how it would be if he were there with me at the Gibralfaro Palace in Málaga, the ancient Jewish quarter in Sevilla, the mosque in Córdoba, and later, in the gardens of the Alhambra. He had either visited Spain before or researched the highlights of each place and thus was able to place us together in all the most likely locations, and go into great detail describing the sexual intimacies we would enjoy in such exotic, romantic settings!

Earlier in our relationship, I might have felt fleetingly flattered by Martin's effort to keep in touch with me while I was away. After all, he had assured me again and again that I was not like any other patient. "You are SPECIAL. What we are doing is a spiritual experiment, and we are making psychological history, like Freud and Jung." Each time I read yet another blatantly transparent seduction, I got furious, recognizing it as his way of keeping me bound to him and preventing me from connecting with anyone else!

I arrived in Granada on my fifth day in Spain. When I checked my mail, there was yet another letter from Martin waiting for me. This time I decided it would be the last one I would read and tore it up. I wanted my stay to be as uncontaminated by my real life as possible. Before we moved to Spain so long ago, I had not yet incurred God's wrath. I wanted to return to that innocent state of grace for just a little while.

I had breakfast in the small *Hostal de Los Angeles* where I rented a room on the second floor, then ventured out to explore the city. I wanted to leave its most famous attraction, the Alhambra, for the afternoon, when the setting sun would make its massive walls glow like shining pomegranate kernels because it was built with the red clay that gave the city of Granada its name. I bought a French newspaper, read it while savoring a bowl of iced *gazpacho* and a roll in a small café, and then walked up the tree-lined street to the fabled fortress-palace created by Arab artisans and architects in the seventh century.

As I stood, awestruck, marveling at the still well-preserved, lace-like patterns applied and carved into the stucco walls of one of the smaller palace rooms, looking up at the intricate swirls of Arabic script inscribed in a border just under the ceiling, a voice right behind me began to whisper in French. I turned around and found myself facing a tall, elegant, dark man dressed in a white linen suit.

"*Vous parlez français, non?*" he asked, pointing to the newspaper under my arm. I nodded.

"*Tous ça, ce sont des verses du Koran,*" he explained, pointing to the carved script on the ceiling border. "I hope you don't mind my translation, but you seemed to be interested."

His name was Abdellatif and he bore an uncanny resemblance to Harry Belafonte. Clearly a well-educated Arab, he proved almost as fluent in English as in French. Although Morocco's official tongue is Arabic, French is its business and diplomatic language.

"You know, this is where our King Boabdil surrendered to Queen Isabella and King Ferdinand in 1492," he told me as we continued to walk through the palace rooms and patios. "That ended my people's seven hundred years of political, cultural, and artistic presence in Spain."

He asked if he might walk along with me. I was pleased to have company after spending the past few days mostly alone. As we proceeded together through the lush Alhambra gardens, cooled by the mist of many fountains we passed along the way, he told me he was a member of the Moroccan government. The Moroccan royal family had a reputation of peaceful co-existence with Jews, so I felt I had no reason to be concerned. Abdellatif also volunteered that he was married to a French doctor who was visiting her family in Paris while he explored Spain.

"We take vacations separately. It is good for marriage to have a little time alone…. It keeps mystery alive."

We spent the evening wandering through the rest of the palace and gardens and had a late dinner on the patio of the *Parador de San Francisco*, a former monastery, now an antiques-filled, government-run, tourist inn right on the Alhambra grounds, offering a spectacular view of old Granada. Just below stood the quaint but stately Washington Irving Hotel, now slightly musty, named after the famous author of the *Tales of the Alhambra*, who was U.S. Ambassador to Spain from 1842–1845.

Since my hostel was not too far for a leisurely walk, Abdellatif offered to accompany me. That gave us an extra hour to spend together and get better acquainted. He told me he had actually come north with a colleague, another member of the Moroccan government, but had convinced him to spend the rest of their stay exploring Spain separately.

"It is hard to meet people when someone else is with you. My compatriot's interests are very different from mine. He is very powerful, and it would not have been healthy for me to offend him. I had to be very diplomatic to be rid of him."

"May I bring you to your room?" Abdellatif asked when we arrived at my hostel. Ignoring a little voice telling me I was playing with fire, I said "Yes, but only for a minute."

As soon as we entered the lobby, the *concierge*, an elderly woman wearing a fringed and colorfully embroidered *manton*, appeared to greet us.

"*Solamente una persona en la habitación*," she announced sternly, waving "no" with her finger as she looked at my companion. Arabs, usually poor illegal immigrants looking for work, were not welcome and often looked upon with suspicion by many people in Spain, especially in the south.

"*Si, Señora. Entiendo,*" I assured her. "*El señor se va en muy pocos minutos.*"

The French doors of my room opened onto a narrow balcony enclosed by a wrought iron railing overlooking a small, walled patio. A colorfully tiled fountain stood in the middle, surrounded by dozens of red clay pots filled with multi-hued flowers. Clusters of purple wisteria stretched up from the garden below—winding around the railing, clinging to the trellis leaning against the wall—reached up to the veranda above mine, where they hung down in a shower of fragrant blossoms. In the distance, the Alhambra, lit by floodlights from the gorge below the towering fortress walls, glowed like an enchanted castle made of garnets floating in the sky. Guitar music wafted back and forth from different directions, carried by a soft breeze.

Abdellatif and I stood there, silently, taking in the magic. Slowly, gently, as though looking for the tiniest sign of tension, he drew me towards him and looked into my eyes. When I closed them to steady myself, suddenly feeling faint, he gently kissed me. I lingered in his embrace, and when I responded by wrapping my arms around him, his own tightened their hold, and his kiss became more passionate. I loved his spicy smell, his strong body molding itself to mine, and felt myself tremble as I let go what little remained of any resistance.

He finally held me at arm's length.

"Please do not misunderstand. I just rented a room with a window looking out on *une petite plaza* not far from here. It is right above *un charmant petit restaurant* called *Allegría*. It has room for two. *S'il te plaît, viens avec moi.* I don't want it all to end here."

Despite his warning, I was somewhat taken aback. "Who does he think I am," I fleetingly wondered, "ready to shack up with a total stranger?"

"We are both married," I murmured. "I'd have to be a little crazy.... I don't even know you."

But then I saw the look in his eyes, eager, serious, even a little sad, and realized I liked this stranger, this Arab. In the little time we had spent together, he impressed me with his gentle, respectful manners, and I suddenly felt I really wanted to be with him, to continue this adventure, anything to blot out my own life at home for even a little while, to prove to myself I could act on my own without anyone else's approval or permission, to surrender to fate, even if it might turn out to be a little reckless and possibly dangerous.

"Yes, I want to be with you," I heard myself whisper, "but not tonight. Tell me where, and I will meet you tomorrow."

As he held me close, a knock on the door broke the spell.

"*Señorita, el señor...!*"

"*Si, si, por favor, ahora mismo...*"

Abdellatif pulled out a small business card embossed with a gold crest and lines of Arabic script and wrote the address where I was to meet him next morning at ten. He gave me a quick hug, walked out, returned to kiss me hard on the mouth, and disappeared.

I sank into bed, and wrapped my arms around myself to recreate the warmth of Abdellatif's embrace. My pounding heart kept me awake till early morning. When I rose up to get a drink of water and looked into the mirror above the small washbasin, I saw my eyes were smiling. I blushed, feeling like the fifteen-year-old girl I was when I first met Nico, twenty-two years ago.

I returned to bed and fell into a deep sleep. When I finally awoke, it was nine thirty. "Oh, it's too late," I thought, half-sad, half-relieved. I shrugged. "He won't be there anyway. I feel like a fool. How stupid of me to think..."

By ten o'clock, I had talked myself into believing the whole episode was just one of those crazy things, a sudden impulse that, if followed, would have brought only embarrassment, disappointment, and regret. How smart of me to have refused to go with Abdellatif last night! I decided to put it all out of my mind. I had missed breakfast at the hostel, so I took my camera, map, and guidebook, ducked into the nearest coffee bar, stood at the counter, dunked a sweet *churro* into a demitasse of strong *café solo*, and set out to explore the rest of Granada.

I was eager to visit the famous Moorish quarter's flea market, where traditional artifacts of the region—lavish embroideries, colorful ceramics, pierced metal lamps with multicolored glass panels, intricately inlaid wood instruments, and dangly Arab-style filigree jewelry—were displayed in stalls manned by gypsies and local artists and craftsmen. Street urchins with baskets hung from their necks were hawking nuts, dates, and flowers. Sweet-smelling, fennel-flavored sausages and other less identifiable delicacies were roasting over coal beds in brass braziers set on burro-driven carts. Taste-samples of dried fruit, olives, and *turron*, the region's traditional almond-studded jawbreaker nougat, were offered to easily tempted tourists. Jars of honey, jam, and spicy sauces were stacked on blankets laid out on the ground. Black lace *mantillas* hung draped over wires above tarp-covered stalls, and large, curlicued, fake tortoise-shell combs to hold them in place lay below in shallow wicker baskets.

In the center of the market stood several large trees, surrounded by small wrought-iron tables and chairs set up in their shade. As soon as I sat down, a waiter from a nearby restaurant appeared.

"*Tapas, señorita?*"

I nodded. "*Si, por favor, y una media botella de vino tinto.*"

While waiting to be served, I closed my eyes and cooled my flushed face with the small, battery-powered, plastic fan I had bought before I left Los Angeles. I looked up when a loud chatter around me roused me from my reverie. A small girl pointed to my fan and begged her mother to get her one like it.

"*Ven aquí, mona, toma lo,*" I motioned to the child.

When the mother brought over her daughter, I offered to let her try out my mechanical contraption. The child squealed with delight when I showed her how to turn it on and off and ran off with it to show to her little friends.

The mother became embarrassed.

"*Señorita, desculpe por favor,*" she apologized. "*Quiere el mío??*" she asked, offering to trade her exquisite traditional black and gold silk fan for my modern wind robot. I gladly accepted.

My wine and *tapas* finally arrived, little oval plates, each with a different delicacy: tiny sardines crispy-fried in olive oil; thin slices of *jamón Serrano*, the Spanish-style, prosciutto-like ham, wrapped around chunks of nutty *Manchego* cheese; black and green olives; tiny marinated clams and *angulas*, baby eels deep fried to look like spaghetti swimming in a garlicky tomato sauce. As I took my time tasting one delectable dish after another, I suddenly looked up to see Abdellatif standing beside me.

First he looked stricken. Then he smiled.

"I found you! I waited for you. A long time. Then I went looking for you. And now here you are."

I covered my face in embarrassment. How could I tell him the truth? He looked stricken.

"I'm sorry," I finally blurted out, "I did not think you were serious. I was afraid, I felt foolish, certain you would not be there...."

"Why would you believe that when..." His voice drifted off.

"You must have lived many sad experiences for you to feel so little trust," he whispered as he sat down next to me. "Come, let me help you wipe out those bad dreams." I invited him to share the rest of my *tapas* and wine before we took off to retrieve my belongings.

The *concierge* was not at her desk when we returned to my hostel. I retrieved my passport from the mail cubbyhole behind the reception desk, left enough *pesetas* to cover my bill on the counter, and let Abdellatif carry my suitcase. As I followed him through the narrow, winding cobble streets, the intoxicating fragrance of jasmine mingled with the pungent aroma of olive oil, garlic, coffee, and cinnamon along the way. Suddenly the street opened up onto a small plaza surrounded by balconied buildings with straw sticking out in between the red tiles of their roofs. Sidewalk cafés, providing respite to tired shoppers, shared the space around its periphery.

"There, look," Abdellatif said, pointing up to a sign on the roof of a three-story-tall building with flowers and ivy covering the whole façade, climbing all the way to the top above the row of umbrella-shaded chairs and tables.

"*Hotel La Alegría*," he whispered. "Joy! That is what I feel now that I have found you. Come, let me show you my room."

I followed him up three narrow flights of stairs, and he opened a bright blue door to a sun-drenched room with deep orange walls. Yellow molding defined a high, vaulted ceiling. Double wood-shuttered doors led out to a flower-bedecked balcony overlooking the plaza below. The furniture was sparse and rustic: against one wall stood a small, carved wooden desk and a chair painted yellow with little blue stars. On the opposite side, two sets of three-armed candelabra with half-burned red candles were nailed to the wall with a ring of soot behind them. Below them stood a wrought-iron stand just large enough to accommodate a blue and white striped ceramic basin and a matching jug filled with water. A copper-framed mirror hung above it at eye-level between the candelabra.

There were two pictures on the other walls: one was of the *Virgen de la Macarena*, the bullfighters' patron saint, resplendent in one of the many richly bejeweled capes she wears during holy week processions in Sevilla. The other showed a couple of fiery flamenco dancers, bodies arched, arms raised and scowling at each other. In the middle of the room stood a carved wood, four-poster bed covered with a yellow tapestry spread enclosed by a filmy mosquito net attached to the ceiling.

He looked at me. "Well, how do you like my magic room?" he asked, enfolding me in his arms. "You will see, you will dream only good dreams here, I promise."

Abdellatif kept his promise. That room became our safe haven to which we returned again and again during the seven days we spent together. He rented a car, and we explored several of the tiny, white-washed villages tucked into the mountain crevices above Granada. We tasted as many new dishes as we could find on the *cantina* menus and kept cool by drinking strong, citrusy *sangría*.

Since I was a virgin when I was married at nineteen, and the only other man aside from my husband with whom I had had sex was Martin, it took me a while to let myself surrender completely to Abdellatif, but once I did, I found him to be a most considerate as well as highly erotic lover, full of delicious surprises: jasmine blossoms on my pillow, massages with fragrant oils. We shared exotic sexual fantasies that often left us both limp with laughter as well as breathless after succumbing to the arousal they generated. I felt pampered, completely cared for, by turns wildly tingling with sexual energy and peacefully spent.

When he encouraged me to share some private aspects of my life, I felt safe enough to reveal some of them. He made me feel understood, accepted. When I told him I was a Jew, he casually reminded me of something he assumed was common knowledge: that Moroccans had a long history of peaceful coexistence with Jews, that the royal court routinely had Jewish guests, and that he himself had many Jewish friends.

He described his own life as busy with responsibilities as a minister in the Moroccan government that required spending a lot of time at the royal court. A close friend of King Hassan's sister, Princess Lalla, he regularly joined her to play tennis on the palace grounds. As was the custom at that time, his own marriage had been arranged, but he had resisted familial and religious pressure and married a non-Moslem woman whom he met when she visited Rabat to attend a medical conference. They had no children although both had hoped to start a family, but after fourteen years that dream had been long abandoned.

"My wife is a very interesting woman. We love one another, we are each other's best friends, but we live mostly separate lives," he explained.

The week we spent together was wonderfully healing. By the time we had to go our separate ways, he to return to Morocco, and I to proceed north, it was hard for both of us to say good-bye. Abdellatif took me to the bus I was to take to Madrid and sat with me, silently, holding my hand, until it was ready to depart.

He then wrapped his arms around me and whispered in my ear: "The one thing I regret is that we will not have a child together."

I smiled at his willingness to openly express this romantic fantasy, knowing that both of us realized that our entire time together belonged in a dream-like province of the heart and remained no less real for it. Then, as the bus began to move, he kissed me hard, jumped off, and waved to me until I could no longer see him.

We corresponded for the next three years, sweet letters in French full of shared memories and delicious fantasies of what might-have-been. When the Arabs attacked Israel in 1967, his letters abruptly stopped. It must have been too risky for him to be caught corresponding with anyone in a country that supported Israel.

2

DARK TIME in MADRID

All the way to Madrid I felt warm and weepy, wrapped in an imaginary goose-down puff. I slept part of the way. I needed those few hours to let go of the magic, to enable me to focus on the task ahead: find a place to stay in Madrid, a huge, bustling metropolitan city, lacking all the southern gentility of Andalusia I had gotten used to. All I saw on arrival in Madrid were wide avenues lined with massive apartment buildings, no Moorish architecture, no narrow cobble-stoned alleys along flower-bedecked courtyards or inner patios with gurgling fountains behind thick outer walls. I felt intimidated, alone, lost, and desperately missed Abdellatif.

A cabby suggested I stay at the inexpensive, mid-city, two-star-rated *Hostal San Antonio* (room, shared bath, and continental breakfast), occupying the second and third floors of an office building on the *Gran Vía*, Madrid's main artery, with good bus service at the door. I took the rickety elevator to the check-in desk on the second floor and looked over my room one floor up. It appeared clean, simple but utilitarian, and, since I planned to spend minimal time indoors, I decided to try staying there for two nights.

By the time I had checked in, unpacked, and hung up my clothes, it was past noon. I was hungry, but the only restaurant I could find open for lunch was a hamburger joint called *El Dólar*, clearly catering to American tourists. One of the lovely Spanish traditions still practiced in the sixties was the *siesta*: it encouraged people to enjoy a mid-day break as well as ample time to meet with friends for a leisurely late lunch, before once again returning to work from four to eight or even nine o'clock. Dinner started no sooner than ten o'clock and often lasted well past midnight.

This delightful, socially-oriented custom has been eroded over time as Spain joined the rest of the emerging world competing for commercial success. Now major stores are open seven days a week, and *siestas* last no longer than an Ameri-

14

can lunch hour. But back in 1964, all businesses closed down from noon to four, as well as all day on Sundays and holidays, and most restaurants did not open for lunch until around two o'clock.

Because there were no English-language newspapers at the nearest *kiosk*, I picked up a French periodical and ordered a cheeseburger and fries at *El Dólar* It all tasted greasy and overdone, especially unpleasant after getting used to authentic Spanish cuisine for so many days. I ate only a part of the meal, made a quick exit, and started walking up the avenue, feeling disoriented and miserable. All I wanted to do was go up to my room, sleep, and forget where I was.

Just as I was about to cross the street to my hostel, a very dark man dressed in a pale blue silk suit with a diamond stickpin in his white tie caught up with me.

"Vous êtes française?" he asked, pointing to my French newspaper. I now recalled noticing him sitting at a nearby table at *El Dólar*, and he must have followed me out. How odd, I thought. This is just how I met Abdellatif.

"No. Je suis americaine."

"Ah, mais vous parlez français!"

He now proceeded to tell me how alone he felt in a city where no one spoke French, and how happy he was to have encountered me. He told me he was a member of the Moroccan government and asked if I would consent to have dinner with him.

As he spoke, I now remembered Abdellatif telling me he had come to Spain with a colleague, and how diplomatic he had to be to be rid of him. Clearly, this must be the person! What an incredible coincidence!

I was so glad to make contact with someone who knew Abdellatif that I accepted his invitation. After all, it was only for dinner. When I told him my hostel was across the street, and that I needed to take a nap, he agreed:

"Yes, you need to be rested. You will see. I will plan a wonderful evening for us. I shall pick you up at ten-thirty, and we will first go to my favorite restaurant for dinner."

After he left me at the *concierge* desk, I walked up one flight to my room and collapsed into a deep sleep. I awoke at about ten and rushed to put on the one really dressy outfit that was not too badly wrinkled: a pale blue silk shirt, matching long skirt, gold spikey sandals, and gold straw clutch.

As I transferred my make-up and other essentials from my travel pouch to my clutch, I realized I had used up nearly all my Spanish pesetas and would have to go to the bank first thing in the morning to cash in some of my traveler's checks. I felt somewhat uncomfortable at the thought that, since the *concierge* had taken my passport as security, I would have nothing on me to identify me officially.

At ten-thirty sharp, the *concierge* rang my phone:

"*Señorita, un señor está aquí esperando,*" she announced.

I walked down to the lobby, and there was my dinner date, resplendent in a white silk suit, diamond cuff links, bare feet under white patent leather loafers, a red silk handkerchief in his breast pocket, and a matching ascot at his neck. He also brought along a white orchid corsage he insisted on pinning to my blouse. How different from Abdellatif, I thought with a slight twinge, he who had been so casual and unpretentious, so easy to be with. I picked up a hostel business card just in case I forgot the address and greeted my gentleman caller.

"How exquisite you look," he gushed. "I decided to let my chauffeur go. We will use taxis. Come, I have left one waiting downstairs."

He directed the driver to take us to *Casa Valentin*, an exclusive garden restaurant at the bottom of a hill, some distance away from the city center. I had read about it in a Madrid travel guide and remember it being described as among the best and very expensive. The entrance to *Casa Valentin* was an ornate bronze gate set in a high stucco wall surrounding the entire property. Inside, all the tables were spaced amidst huge clay pots filled with flowers, each candle-lit and covered with red table linens and bright poppy-embossed china. Overhead were row upon row of accordion-pleated, blue canvas cover strips, tightly folded but ready to be extended over the restaurant garden and its guests to provide shade or protection against the slightest sign of rain. The lobby, kitchen, and other amenities were housed in a long structure along the wall, next to the entry gate.

The maître d' immediately recognized my date, addressed him as *Vôtre Majesté Ministre Musaf*," and with great flourish showed him to our table at the far end of the patio. When our waiter came to offer him the menu card, Musaf refused to even look at it and, without consulting me, began to order all sorts of exotic-sounding Arabic dishes that were unknown to me. He was very specific about how he expected each item to be prepared, and the waiter was barely able to keep up writing down his directions. Musaf also ordered the best champagne available.

"I know what to order," he noted as soon as the waiter was gone. "You will love everything, I guarantee it."

I must admit I was impressed but quite intimidated. I also felt irritated and uneasy with Musaf's insistence on making all decisions for both of us without consulting me. I remembered that Abdellatif sometimes took the initiative, but his choices were sweet and gentle guesses based on what he had observed, and he always made sure I approved and gave me the option to refuse or to change my mind. I never needed to.

Something about Musaf kept me from mentioning Abdellatif's name, although I was certain he was the government colleague he had mentioned. Alone in Madrid, I was at first so happy to make a connection with someone, anyone, even peripherally connected to Abdellatif, I now began to remember something in his voice when he mentioned his compatriot that I should have recognized as dislike. Now that dislike began to affect me, too, I found myself afraid of some amorphous, intangible threat I could not quite define. While waiting for the waiter to bring our food, Musaf kept refilling my champagne flute again and again, well before I had emptied it. Even after I tried to cover the glass and admitted that I was not used to taking more than two drinks at most, he dismissed my protests. "Don't worry, you can't get drunk on this special vintage."

Even through a growing mental haze, I could see that Musat was attempting to distract me with minute details of his personal life in Rabat while plying me with increasingly intoxicating champagne. He casually mentioned that he had four wives.

"Many Moroccan men no longer feel the need for multiple wives, but I see it a perfect solution to my rather...(here he hesitated, smiling, as he searched for the right word) *particular* appetites. No one woman could possibly satisfy me."

He went on and on, telling me he had many children and lived in an opulent palace, which was frequently used for lavish parties. When I did not respond with the proper degree of astonishment, he pulled out a packet of photos to prove that nothing he told me was exaggerated. Then the conversation took an even more bizarre turn. He began to describe various sexual practices he had learned to enjoy. They included orgies with simultaneous multiple partners, male as well as female, bondage, sado-masochism, even use of children and animals.

"Have you ever been brave enough to try any of these adventures?" he wanted to know. "I am fascinated by the dark side of human sexuality. It brings an almost god-like power to any participant, the feeling that no experience is beyond our grasp. Nothing is outside the realm of possibility."

By now I was not only sick to my stomach but also terrified. The food arrived, but I was unable to eat. He kept forcing me to try this and that, and, though I had become dizzy and felt I might vomit any moment, there was no way I could escape his pressure. While he ate with undiminished relish, as each of the many dishes came and went, all I could think of was how I could get away. The fact that no one at home knew where I was, or with whom, and that I had virtually no money nor identification on me, only increased my panic. I don't know how long we had been at *Valentin's*, but I now noticed that most of the other tables were empty. Many of the candles illuminating the place had been extinguished. I looked at my watch. Two thirty in the morning!

"Monsieur, I have a terrible headache. Please take me back to the hostel."

"Oh, my dear, it's much too early," he protested. "The night is still young, and we must go to my favorite club to dance. You would not deprive me of this pleasure, would you?"

Now all kinds of monstrous fantasies ran through my mind.

"My God," I thought, "I could disappear without a trace into Musaf's harem, and no one would ever find me!" I knew I had to act, NOW.

"Please excuse me," I said getting up, "but I must use the bathroom. I will be right back." I grabbed my purse, and, before Musaf could protest, I unsteadily wove my way through the maze of tables and entered the main building where the *servicios* were located. A large, middle-aged woman wearing a maid's cap and uniform with a long, white apron covering her black skirt, sat at the bathroom entrance. She rose to unlock the toilet and held out her hand for her customary gratuity.

"Señora," I whispered, *"Por favor, ayudame. Soy con un hombre muy malo, muy peligroso. Tengo mucho miedo!* He is sitting at a table in the back there. I have to get away immediately. He must not see me leave. Please please help me!"

The woman looked at me, wide-eyed. Then she grabbed one of my hands and said. *"No se preocupe. Dios va ayudarnos.* (Do not worry. God will help us)." Now she spread out her long skirt and told me to crouch down behind her. "Follow me out to the gate," she commanded. "I will hide you. No one will see you." Slowly, inching our way along the long, dark wall, we safely reached the exit gate and rushed outside. The uniformed guard who had greeted Musaf and me earlier was still on duty.

"Oye, José" she began, spilling out my story in agitated staccato, gesticulating wildly and pointing down at the patio rear.

José smiled. *"María, no te apurres,"* he told the woman and assured her she could leave me to his care. María and I hugged as I whispered my thanks. When she disappeared inside the gate, José turned to me. *"Señorita, venga conmigo."*

He took my hand and pulled me up the hill to a street with only a modicum of traffic. He shoved me into an apartment doorway while trying to flag down a taxi that failed to materialize. Now I suddenly heard the sound of heavy footsteps approaching from the bottom of the hill.

I rushed out to José. *"Por favor!* He is following me!" I whispered. "We must get away from here!"

"There are more taxis on the next *avenida*," he said, pulling me up another two blocks. With my heart pounding, I watched as José finally succeeded in attracting a cab.

"Get in, *Señorita*," he commanded, then explained my predicament to the driver. I scrambled to find what little money I had on me, but José refused to take it.

"It is my pleasure to help a lady," he said, "May God help you reach safety."

We took off hurriedly, and I finally breathed a sigh of relief as we approached the *Gran Vía*. When we reached my hostel, I once more offered the cabby what little change I had on me, and once more, like José, he gallantly refused to accept any of it.

"We Spanish want our visitors to remember us with pleasure. I am glad to help a lady in distress. Like *Don Quixote!*"

I thanked him, and, as he drove off, I rushed to the front door of the hostel. The street was nearly deserted when I discovered that the wrought-iron gate, that had earlier been open to provide easy access to the interior and its elevators, was now chained with a padlock! All I could think of, as my panic raged and nearly paralyzed me, was that Musaf knew where to find me. I knew it was only a matter of minutes before he would catch up with me. I began to rattle the gate wildly, hoping someone inside would hear the racket and come to my rescue.

Suddenly an elderly man, dressed in medieval-looking garb, emerged from the dark, holding up a large brass ring with dozens of keys.

"*Señorita. Yo soy el sereno. Yo tengo todos los llaves para aquí.* I have all the keys for buildings in this area. It is for *seguridad.* When you clap your hands, I come to open your door. Here, let me help you." He unlocked the gate and secured it again after me. Once safely inside, I bounded up the flight of stairs to the hostel lobby. The same *concierge* was at the desk.

"*Por favor, escuche me bien,*" I pleaded. "If the same *señor* comes here looking for me do not let him in. Tell him I am not here." She told me not to worry and handed me my key. I rushed up to the next floor, locked the door behind me, and pulled the bedcovers over my head without even getting undressed.

About fifteen minutes later, my phone rang. "*Señorita*, the *señor* was here, the one that was here before. He wanted me to call you. When I said you were not here, he left a large basket full of fruit and a bottle of champagne and a bouquet of roses and said he would come back for you later."

"*Muchísimas gracias, señora!*" I answered. "Please keep the flowers and the basket with everything in it for yourself, prepare my bill, and have my passport ready. Call another hostel, any hostel away from the city center, make a reservation for me, and then call a taxi."

She carefully followed all my instructions and also broke all kinds of regulations to exchange one of my American traveler's checks for *pesetas*. Like the other three good Samaritans who had agreed to help me and show me the kindness and hospitality of which Spain is rightfully proud, she took only the amount I owed, refused to accept any gratuity, and wished me well.

I spent the next three days cooped up in a tiny room somewhere in a Madrid suburb, afraid to go anywhere. Until I finally decided it was safe for me to emerge from hiding to continue my journey, I kept looking back over my shoulder to make sure Musaf was nowhere in sight. Eventually I was able to take a train for Barcelona, looking forward to rediscovering the one place on earth that held only wonderful memories for me.

3

NICO

At first, my stay in Barcelona felt as healing as I had hoped. Familiar places were there just as I remembered them. But this time neither *Señora* Carron nor Pilar were there to welcome me, and I felt lonely, sad that, as I rediscovered my most beloved city on earth, there was no one there to share my joyful nostalgia. Despite those feelings, I took my time to explore all the places I recalled loving so many years ago, retracing my steps to my childhood haunts, where I had lived, played, and gone to school.

By the time I left for home, I had reconnected to Barcelona's spellbinding aura. I felt ready, able to look at life with a somewhat fresh new perspective. I had experienced magic and survived danger. I was certain my romantic adventure in Granada with Abdellatif had a liberating effect on me, proving I could act independently, make decisions, enjoy sex with another man, and feel happy, relaxed, and free. Curse or no curse, I discovered that I could at least experience a temporary reprieve. I now found my thoughts turning back to my first love.

When Nico and I met, I was at first determined to keep from him most of my hidden past and my secret plan for the future. What I did not reveal to him until much later was that my family and I had escaped death during the Holocaust—when we fled from France to Spain as hastily baptized Catholics after war broke out in 1939. My parents had carefully hidden our true identities from my brother and me until just before we left Paris for Barcelona. Although I grew up without any religious or spiritual guidelines, I had early on read about heroes and heroines who were willing to die for the truth. So, lying—pretending I was Catholic when I really was Jewish—felt so wrong that I was certain I had forever forfeited the right to call myself a Jew, whatever that meant.

Then, while living in Spain, I fell under the seductive spell of Catholicism's intoxicating rituals and comforting promises of salvation. Hearing over and over again that Jesus, a Jew, had died to wipe away my sins, I gladly accepted the church's assurance of forgiveness. Later, safe in America by then, I attended a convent boarding school to which a Catholic refugee organization had secured a scholarship for me.

Even before I graduated, concentration camp horror stories turned from mere rumors to reality. Now the denial of my true identity and the fact that I was surviving the war by fraud, when so many Jews were being murdered, became in my mind a major crime for which forgiveness seemed unattainable. Thus, at the age of fifteen, I felt damned, ashamed of my betrayal, and hoped to atone for my masquerade by forgoing a normal life. I vowed to become a Maryknoll missionary nun and planned to enter their novitiate after college graduation. I hoped God would accept my sacrifice and forgive me. If I ended up dying a martyr's death in some faraway place, so be it.

Then I fell in love with Nico. The resulting spiritual conflict plunged me into turmoil.

◆   ◆   ◆

Nico first appeared in my life the last summer weekend before I was due to return to Marycliff Academy for my senior year. I was visiting a classmate whose family lived in Asbury Park. While she attended to personal matters, I was glad to escape the August heat at the city's beautiful, old, public swim club. As I stood poised, my toes curled under the edge of the high diving board, debating whether I could muster the courage to take the plunge, someone crept up behind me and pushed me in. When the sneaky perpetrator splashed in right after me, I lunged at him, bent on murder.

"You stupid! You could have drowned me!"

"Naa. You're a good swimmer," he said with a grin, "I've been watching you. You just needed a little shove."

As he held me at arm's length, fending off my flailing fists, my rage quickly turned to laughter. By the time he pulled me out of the water and wrapped his towel around me, my fury had dissipated. How could anyone stay angry at such a splendid creature! Tall, trim, toned, and tanned, with a shock of wet black hair dripping into dark eyes, a broad smile flashing perfect teeth, he looked like the very incarnation of a Greek god standing there, glistening golden-hued in the sun. That was even before I knew Nico actually was Greek.

At first, we sat with our feet dangling in the pool and talked. He told me his family owned a popular restaurant in Chicago where he and his brothers and sisters used to wash dishes after school during their teens. His was a large, typically close-knit family, deeply involved with their neighborhood Greek Orthodox Church where Nico had sung in the choir since he was a boy. Although he was open and eager to talk about his life, when he asked about mine, I was careful not to reveal too many details. Still, we ended up speaking with an oddly intense intimacy, the way one shares secrets with a stranger one never expects to meet again.

"You have a cute accent," he said. "Where are you from?"

"I grew up in Europe, and my family came to America two years ago."

We spent the rest of that afternoon walking along the boardwalk. When the sun set behind the New York skyline, Nico offered to bring me back to my friend's home on the back of his motorcycle.

"Where do you live?" he wanted to know. "And can I have your phone number?"

"I am a student at a boarding school near Boston. That's where I am most of the time. But my parents live in Manhattan. I do occasionally go home on weekends," I added.

"It's too bad we live so far apart," he whispered as he hugged me good-bye. I was sure that fate had capriciously thrown us together on that small spot on the Jersey shore for just that one magical moment in time. Although he promised to call, I was certain I would never hear from him again. But he did call.

During my first two years away at school, I had hardly ever gone home. Home was a war-zone much of the time. Mama and Papa were at odds about just about everything, mostly his inability to find and keep a job, and I was often pulled into the conflict by one or the other and pressured to take sides. School had become my peaceful refuge.

"I need to practice my English," was the excuse I had given my parents for staying away. But when I found out that Nico could get away most weekends, I decided to risk going home, hoping that having an outsider around would force them to defer their battles until I was safely back at school.

Real privacy was hard to find. But in those days, it was still safe to walk in Central Park and find a secluded spot to spread out a blanket on the grass. Many a Saturday night, I lay with my head in Nico's lap as he leaned against a tree, looking up to the stars and wishing time would stand still.

Most often we went down to nearby Riverside Drive and walked along the Hudson, just getting to know one another. Other times, I packed a basket full of goodies for a leisurely picnic, or we went to the zoo, explored small ethnic restaurants, or listened to live jazz till early morning at some Greenwich Village club.

I soon discovered that Nico was very well read and had a deeply spiritual side. I found him to be remarkably knowledgeable about philosophy and various religions, including Judaism. Both Nico and I enjoyed classical music and spent many a summer night at Lewisohn Stadium for concert and opera performances. He loved opera, had a lovely voice, and dreamed of singing in an operatic chorus.

In winter, skating in Rockefeller Plaza's ice rink, I was able to show off the figure-skating skills I had learned as a child on ice-covered tennis courts along the *Vltava* River in Prague as a student of teen-aged Vera Hruba. Later she became Sonia Henie's unsuccessful rival, not only competing for Olympic gold, but also for Hollywood stardom, having to settle for RKO's B-movie queen's crown as Vera Hruba Ralston in westerns—and as the studio boss' wife. I would not have traded places with either Sonia or Vera; I was glowing with pride as Nico knelt at my knees to lace up my skates, feeling other skaters smiling at us as they slid by. Nico was an expert dancer, and wherever he swung me up and around, doing a wild jitterbug, other couples would spontaneously leave the floor to watch us and applaud.

For special occasions, Nico sometimes took me dancing to Tavern on the Green in Central Park, its trees all lit up with tiny, twinkling lights and a real live orchestra playing under the stars. On many a moonlit night, we danced to slow music, barely moving, just letting our bodies sway to the lazy rhythm as Nico held me close. Often the evening would end with a horse-drawn carriage ride, the horses trotting leisurely all around the park, while we cuddled in privacy under the shawl the driver had provided.

Although most of the time Nico accompanied me to Sunday mass, one year he invited me to attend Easter services in New York's Greek Orthodox Cathedral. I felt a little uneasy at first, but we solved that problem by going to early mass and communion in my parish church first. Finding me all dressed up in a pale pink, linen Easter suit with a wide-brimmed straw hat I decorated with a bunch of pink baby roses tucked into a green, gros-grain bow, Nico beamed as he pinned a gardenia corsage to my suit collar.

The candle-lit interior of the cathedral—the shimmering, gold-encrusted icons on every wall, the pageantry of the large contingent of festively robed celebrants at the altar, and the rousing choir—were all as memorable and moving as anything I had ever experienced in Spain's churches. But as the services went on for more than two hours, the effect of the intoxicating incense filling the sanctuary mixed with my gardenia corsage's overwhelming fragrance soon became too much. By the time everyone finally rose to leave, I swooned like an opera diva between two pews, and Nico ended up having to carry me out where the fresh air quickly revived me.

While all this made me feel ever more close to Nico, I was constantly torn by guilt, trying to honor my vow to prepare myself for a religious life while aching to be with Nico, whom I was still determined to keep in the dark about my secret plan, not ready to give him up. I had long kept a diary into which I poured all my most secret yearnings, as well as my cries for help when nothing seemed to make any sense. My doubts often left me adrift, floating on a deceptively calm sea, while invisible whirlpools suddenly appeared and threatened to suck me down to my doom.

Overwhelmed and lacking someone in whom I could safely confide, desperate to find some balance between the conflicting demands of my emotional, physical, and spiritual needs, I blush now as I read some of the poems that expressed my turmoil as my relationship with Nico became increasingly intense.

TRICKERY

Oh heart of mine, you little witch,
Why do you tell me lies?
Why do you sing that song of love
In which my ruin lies?
You know I care not for the world
Nor for its pleasures gay,
For I have pledged myself to God
One lovely winter day.
I trust not in the song you sing,
That song of sweet enchantment,
For it is in God and God alone
I want to find contentment.
So, hush my heart, but burn with love
For Christ, my soul's real spouse,
Until the day he'll take us both
Up to His father's house.

AMIDST IT ALL

I laugh and play when I go out,
I'm thrilled when I go dancing.
I'm sure I like boys' company,
Enjoy a li'l romancing.
But Jesus, dear, amidst it all
I won't forget thy gracious call.

OUT OF THIS WORLD

He's not much different from the rest
That boy in navy blue,
And I go always plainly dressed
As most respectful young girls do.
And yet how oft do people turn
To see us walking by,
How oft do couples stand aside
To watch us dancing by.
How very often do we feel
That not too far away,
Some curious people try to hear
What he and I will say.
And even when we do not speak
Or utter little sighs,
The smiling crowd still seems to read
The answer in our eyes.
But we don't care the slightest bit
What others think or say,
For in each other's company
The world just fades away.

As Nico and I spent more and more time together, my parents soon learned to look forward to his visits and treated him like a member of the family. They were impressed with his manners and respectful attitude. Mama liked to show off her cooking, and Papa took great pride in beating him at an occasional bridge game.

But Nico and I most looked forward to the times when my parents had afternoon social engagements or matinée tickets to the opera. Alone at last, we were able to let down our guard, and openly express our pent-up passions. We explored each other's bodies like hungry puppies, wrenching apart again and again at that crucial moment when our excitement was just a hair's-breath away from exploding and plunging us into mortal sin. After surviving another such particularly frustrating foray into sexual Russian roulette, breathless and soaked in perspiration, Nico and I rushed outside to cool off.

"Let's dangle our feet in the water," he suggested and climbed over the chain fence separating the Riverside walkway from the Hudson River.

When I tried to follow, I got stuck, with one leg straddling each side of the chain, and Nico had to pick me up and lift me over. We were unable to reach the water with our feet, but the air was cool and pleasant, and we ended up lying down on the grass near Grant's Tomb.

Later that night, after Nico had left to return to his base, I found a note under my pillow: "Oh how I envy the fence!"

By the time Nico was sent overseas, I had made up my mind to spend my life with the man I loved. "I am too young to renounce marriage and live a celibate life," I rationalized, not at all convinced of the validity of my excuse.

After exchanging love-letters filled with plans for our future together for two years, everything suddenly ended. Although I was devastated when Nico did not ask me to marry him on his return from overseas, I was not surprised. When I did not hear from him after he brought his parents to New York to meet me, I knew that losing Nico was my just punishment for lying to stay alive and breaking my vow.

Years later, I found out that Nico had in fact returned after a period of silent adjustment. By the time he called my mother to tell her he was back and wanted to marry me, she told him, "You're too late."

I eventually confronted Mama. "Why did you lie to Nico? You knew I was not yet married!"

Mama became all flustered: "You should thank me! I saved you from a life of grief. You know his family would have hated you for not being Greek. They're worse than Jews!" Mama also never forwarded any of Nico's letters to me. When he chose a wife, four years after I myself had married, it was to a Greek girl. Mama had taken control of my life and done what she thought was best for me. I never quite forgave her for robbing me of the chance to make my own choice, although I secretly wondered if she might not have been right.

When my dream of spending my life with Nico proved to be a cruel illusion, I accepted my fate, certain it was proof that my life would forever be cursed. By then it was 1946, and I was a junior at Manhattanville College of the Sacred Heart in New York, to which I had accepted a scholarship to prepare myself for my secret religious vocation. Although I never totally accepted many of Catholicism's articles of faith, each time I received the sacred host during communion, I was overwhelmed by indescribable feelings of hope, grace, and peace, certain that God was inside me in a most concrete way. Nothing else seemed to matter as much, and this became the primary foundation of my commitment.

Then I suddenly felt compelled to question many Catholic dogmas as I became aware of what seemed to be Church-sanctioned anti-Semitism all around me. I was particularly appalled by the Pope's refusal to intervene on behalf of the persecuted millions being slaughtered by the Nazis. My concerns, openly voiced in class, were seen as nothing less than a defiant, rebellious challenge to the Church's policies and practices and thus were judged a serious threat to the faith of other students. The hostile, defensive reactions and responses by members of the faculty only increased my doubts and my resurging depression. I knew I did not have the right to call myself a Jew, and now I realized I could no longer in good conscience remain a Catholic. Slowly I found myself drifting into a spiritual no-man's land.

One life-altering event occurred before I quit Manhattanville at the end of my junior year: I found out about the medieval *Marranos* while researching a history project. *Marranos*—Jews who chose baptism when the Spanish Inquisition threatened to burn them at the stake if they did not convert—felt they were justified in submitting to baptism, certain God would understand, even approve. What they hid from the church was that they became Catholics IN NAME ONLY, secretly continuing to hold on to their Jewish identities, their laws, and their connection to their Jewish traditions, despite constant danger of betrayal by neighbors or accusations of "judaising" by the Inquisition, often followed by torture and death.

Although at first I felt an instant mystical kinship with the *Marranos*, relieved that there was an acceptable precedent for what my family and I had done, and dreamed of some day returning to Spain—to find some *Marranos* and ask them to teach me to be a Jew—I was afraid that it was too late to comfort myself with their example. I felt I had burned all my spiritual bridges behind me, convinced, at nineteen, that I was beyond forgiveness and salvation forever, and belonged nowhere. Depression nearly paralyzed me.

By the time I quit Manhattanville, becoming a nun was no longer an option. I had also lost Nico. Confused and searching for something to do with my life, I saw and replied to a "help wanted" ad, never dreaming I would be accepted. Without any prior experience, I was hired as a jewelry-design apprentice with one of the most prestigious jewelry houses on Fifth Avenue, whose head designer was impressed with my watercolor rendition of an utterly un-producible diamond pin.

This part-time job accomplished what I hoped it might: it served as a temporary distraction. I let myself get lost in the store's glamorous atmosphere. The entire design staff was housed on the second floor behind a terrace railing overlooking the sales salon below. Two guards armed with Tommy guns, and standing on either side of the balcony, routinely called us to watch whenever such celebrities as Paulette Goddard (dressed in leopard to match the upholstered interior of her foreign convertible parked at the curb) happened to sashay in; or to watch the twin Princes of Bourbon (hired as sales staff to add even greater distinction to the establishment's status) go into near heart-failure watching the Maharaja of Baroda and his Maharani's children play marbles with cabochon emeralds and rubies on the marble showroom floor, while their parents selected millions of dollars' worth of baubles.

Although I learned invaluable techniques of design during my apprenticeship year, which later became the foundation of my three-decade-long career as a jewelry designer, I eventually left this position, partly because my depression worsened, and because I felt uncomfortable with some of the unethical duties I was asked to perform: whenever a famous person wearing an unusual piece of jewelry appeared on the premises, one of the princes would offer to have it cleaned to enhance its brilliance. My job was to keep a pan with a mixture of some kind of wet plaster in the refrigerator and secretly make a cast of the piece before thoroughly cleaning it! This in spite of the presence of thirteen talented designers on the staff!!!

My depression eventually became so severe that I knew I had to get away from everything in New York, especially because everything reminded me of Nico. I felt I belonged nowhere, had no secure identity, no spiritual footing. I was convinced my life was cursed forever, and there was nothing I could do to escape it.

I chose what at the time appeared to be the easiest way out: I impulsively promised to follow a man I barely knew who was about to leave New York to attend graduate school three thousand miles away, in California. He asked me to marry him, and I said yes.

4

MAMA

I was born in what used to be Romania. After World War II, it became part of the Soviet Union and recently evolved into the independent state of Ukraine. My mother, who was born in Vienna, met my father on a visit to his Romanian hometown, Czernovitz. He caught sight of her browsing through his family's pharmacy, was instantly dazzled by her beauty, offered to help her, struck up a conversation, fell in love with her, vigorously pursued her, and convinced her to marry him and move to Romania.

My brother Fredo was born when I was eighteen months old, just after I became ill with streptococcus sepsis. A burst abscess in my throat had poisoned my blood and threatened to kill me. For the next six months, Mama hovered over me, dragging me from doctor to doctor, frantically searching for someone offering a cure at a time when antibiotics had not yet been discovered.

Convinced I was about to die, she took me to a gypsy healer who placed an ancient coin on my forehead and promised I would survive. Many years later, long after Papa revealed we were Jews, Mama admitted it was not a gypsy but a rabbi, whose healing powers she had sought. Actually it was a young doctor from Palestine who brought about the miracle by performing a complicated, never-before-tested, blood exchange from Papa to me that saved my life.

Mama confirmed that my recall of that procedure at such an early age was remarkably accurate: I remember it in clear detail, as though it happened yesterday: Mama holding me tight, her tears wetting my face while she whispered softly to me, as the doctor cut into my wrist in order to insert a coiled glass tube laid out on our round dining room table, with the other end spliced into my father's. Red blood flowed from him through the transparent tube into my vein, and black blood poured from a second cut in my wrist and splashed into a basin at the doctor's feet. All this was done without anesthetic because I had a minor heart murmur.

31

My illness marks my last warm childhood memories of Mama. As soon as I was well enough to travel, our family moved from Czernovitz to Prague. All my familiar surroundings were suddenly gone. Filled with guilt for having completely left my baby brother's care to our nanny during my illness, Mama now made up for her neglect by devoting herself exclusively to him.

Trying to make sense of this sudden abandonment, I concluded she loved my brother more than me because he had a rather large head compared to mine. If only some magic could make my head as big as his, I wished, so Mama would love me again!

My head never grew bigger, and from the time we moved to Prague, my relationship with Mama was never the same.

◆   ◆   ◆

In 1990, when my mother found out that a major publisher would actually publish the memoir I had been working on, she said, "You should be writing MY life story. It's so much more interesting than yours." I immediately sent her an audio-tape machine and blank cassettes, repeatedly pleading with her to record some of the incidents in her life to which she had occasionally obliquely alluded yet failed to share with me, but she never got around to doing it.

Later, when I sent her a few pages from my manuscript that dealt with her own life, hoping she might add some personal details I did not know, she not only refused to help, she demanded I disguise our family name, and particularly her own name, so no one would ever guess she was my mother. She called to tell me, "Just leave me out of it!" and swore she would never read my book. Then she stopped talking to me for a whole year. Whenever I called her, she slammed down the receiver as soon as she heard my voice.

When Simon & Schuster brought out *The Mezuzah in the Madonna's Foot: Oral Histories Exploring Five Hundred Years in the Paradoxical Relationship of Spain and the Jews* in 1993, I found out that Mama had immediately run out to buy the book. After reading it, she decided it was not as bad as she had expected. Then she had a card printed with the name of the book, my name, her name, and under it, "MOTHER OF THE AUTHOR." She next proceeded to run to dozens of bookstores to make sure *The Mezuzah* was prominently displayed in the shop window!

Of course, Mama never told me any of this. My brother Fredo did. One day Mama casually called and re-established contact with me without any explanation, never mentioning my book, acting as though nothing had happened. From then on, we spoke about everything EXCEPT my book. In 1994, after Harper/ San Francisco brought out the paperback edition, after changing the sub-title to *Marranos and Other Secret Jews: A Woman Discovers Her Spiritual Heritage*, I was awarded a prize from the Jewish Book Council in the category of Biography/ Memoir. I received a call from Mama.

"I want you should FAX me a copy of the award," she demanded. My brother had obviously told her about my honor.

"You don't have a FAX," I reminded her.

"There's a FAX place around the corner."

"Mama, it is snowing. What's the big rush? I'll just mail you a copy of the award."

"No, FAX it. NOW! Everyone here is waiting to see the award."

My ears pricked up. For years Mama had been living in a former luxury apartment hotel remodeled into a senior citizen facility whose residents were predominantly Jewish.

"Are you talking to the residents about my book? You never even told me you read it, or that you liked it!"

"I READ IT, AND I DID NOT LIKE IT!!!"

"What's wrong with the book?"

"Everyone here says that if a daughter of theirs wrote such a book, they would die of shame!"

"WHY?" I asked, becoming exasperated.

"Because there's almost nothing in it about me."

My heart melted. Poor Mama. She could not decide if she should be proud of me or ashamed.

"You know, the book was originally six hundred pages long," I explained, "and the editors cut it down by nearly a half. You're probably on the cutting room floor," I consoled her. After that, she told everyone that the deleted pages were all about her!

A veritable force of nature, Mama's overpowering presence, my awe of her energy, her ingenuity, and chutzpah has dominated much of my life. She overcame the kind of circumstances that would have overwhelmed and defeated most anyone else. She actually seemed to thrive under pressure and was energized by conflict.

Mama was seventy-five years old and still working when a strike shut down all public transportation in New York City. Because it took her forty-five minutes by bus and subway to get from her upper Westside apartment to her office in a downtown Manhattan high-rise, I called to ask how she was enjoying her vacation.

"What vacation?" she harrumphed, "I hitchhike. The truckers are the best. They drop me right at the door." She continued to work without missing a day until she was in her mid-eighties. She died last year at the age of ninety-five, without ever having been ill or spending even one day in a hospital until the last month of her life. She had fallen, broken some bones, decided she had lived long enough, stubbornly refused to eat, and ended up in a hospice.

Now that she is gone, I realize more than ever that everything I have achieved, everything I dared to tackle that made my life such a strange mixture of miraculous highs and often terrifying lows (after making some choices without considering the consequences, as well as letting others pass because I was afraid to fail), all of it was due to Mama's powerful influence. Papa loved me. Mama dominated me.

Although Mama was born in Vienna, she moved to Papa's hometown in Romania after they were married. She always looked at least fifteen to twenty years younger than her true age, mostly due to her flawless, creamy complexion, bright blue eyes, and regal bearing. Although her hair had been blond for as far back as I could remember, her photos as a young woman reveal a patrician beauty with dark, wavy hair framing a high forehead, prominent cheekbones defining a perfectly shaped, oval face with an aquiline nose and sensuous lips.

Mama occasionally brought out a faded newspaper clipping. It shows her lounging on the sand at a crowded beach, dressed in a stylish, striped bathing suit, her shapely legs crossed and stretched out before her. "Look, I was just nineteen here," she murmured, her voice tinged with nostalgia, translating the German caption: "Everyone stopped to admire this beach beauty with the red headband."

Because Mama had suffered an attack of Bell's palsy as a small child, she was very self-conscious about the nearly imperceptible sag on the left side of her face when she smiled, but those early photos reveal no trace of it. In each portrait she is elegantly dressed, and several full-length, formal shots show her tall and slim, her long fingers holding either a diaphanous scarf or a long strand of pearls. In my favorite portrait, a sepia-toned, professionally posed photo, she is holding me, at six months old and naked, her face touching mine in a soft embrace. It is the only photo of her showing a hint of a smile.

My earliest memories of Mama are sweet: being cuddled and sung to before going to sleep; outings in the park with Mama insisting on pushing the deep, English style pram while my nanny walked along holding her purse. I clearly remember our thrice-daily eating ritual, when she would go through all manner of contortions to get me to finish every last spoonful of food. Mama's obsession with food had its roots during the First World War, after her beloved father became one of its earliest fatalities, leaving his once moneyed family destitute and often hungry.

Papa made me feel special in the way he showed his love for me. During our years in Prague, he and I spent many memorable "dates" together. On most Saturday mornings, just the two of us went on outings, to Barandov Studios, where movies are produced to this day, to museums, and always ending with lunch at Lipperts, the most famous "automat" restaurant, where every sandwich displayed in its little slot was a culinary work of art.

Although he himself never produced any art, Papa took time to teach me to draw, setting up still life tableaux of fruit bowls and flowers to explain the principles of shadows and perspective. Long after we had emigrated to America, at a time when he felt utterly defeated by living in a country where his professional talents as inventor-engineer had become irrelevant, and his social status filled him with shame, I sent him several blank canvases, brushes, and a set of oil paints for his sixtieth birthday. Within a year, he had a one-man show in a small gallery!

Papa had a compulsive streak that sometimes showed itself in bizarre ways. When I was three years old, he became convinced that I was destined to become another Shirley Temple and ordered some rather suggestive photos made of me to submit to film studios. Another of his obsessions was table etiquette: he made Fredo and me eat our evening meals with heavy dictionaries under each arm to teach us proper manners, and if we dropped one of the books, we were not allowed to finish our dinner or get dessert.

Later in New York, Papa's most cruel act was to moan and groan, pretending to have a heart attack, when I was on the phone talking to Nico. This caused me to hang up and rush to him, only to find Papa flashing a "gotcha" grin. His act always worked, but, although it made me furious, I never dared to ignore it in case it was real. Ironically, although, like Mama, Papa had been healthy most of his life, he collapsed of a massive heart attack while in his doctor's office for a minor infection at only sixty-two.

After leaving Prague, Mama lived most of her life with a perpetual black cloud over her head. No one outside our immediate family had a clue, because she never spoke of her pain to anyone and reserved the manifestation of her inner storm for her immediate family. There was a reason for the black cloud: Mama never forgave herself for failing to convince her own mother to flee with us from

Prague to Paris soon after the *Anschluss*, when the whole world looked away as Hitler annexed Austria in 1938.

That day Papa woke us up in the middle of the night. "We're going away for a while," he told us. "Pack all you can carry." I guessed from Papa's demeanor that this was not going to be a vacation trip, but I was afraid to ask any questions. We took a taxi to *Oma* Jenny's apartment on our way to the train station. "We're going to Paris. Come with us," Mama pleaded.

"Hitler just marched into Vienna. Prague is next," Papa warned her.

"So, what's he going to do with an old lady like me?" *Oma* Jenny asked and refused to leave. "You'll be back in no time," she added.

Mama wept when we left her behind.

After a terrifying trip across Germany, we settled into a small hotel in Paris. Just a few weeks later, one day before *Oma* Jenny's 58th birthday, March 15, the very day Hitler invaded Prague, Mama made one last desperate attempt to get her mother to join us in Paris. It was too late. They saw each other for a brief moment before Mama fled back alone, braving the dangerous train ride through Germany for the third and last time. Long after our letters to her mother were returned, "occupant unknown" stamped under the swastika seal, Mama found out that *Oma* Jenny, along with thousands of others, had been crammed into a cattle train soon after they last saw each other, only to perish in the Theresienstadt concentration camp.

Where others might have reacted with lethargy and depression to these devastating events, Mama's guilt and dark vision energized and mobilized her to sharpen her survival skills. Despite moving from one foreign country to another three times with two small children before she was thirty-six years old, leaving behind everything that meant anything to her, she took charge of our family long before Papa died a broken man at our final destination, New York. Unlike her, he was unable to cope with the loss of status and prestige he had enjoyed as a professional in Prague. While he relieved his shame and depression by gambling, Mama buried her pain under a blur of activity.

The first time Mama took charge of our family was in Paris, where we lived for eighteen months. Because we had left Prague so hurriedly, Papa was only able to take out limited funds. This provided him an excuse for indulging his passion for gambling. He bet on horses and joined high stakes card games, hoping to thus provide money for our family. Accustomed to being in control, he felt lost in a strange country, a foreign refugee unable to speak the local language, too proud to accept jobs he deemed beneath him. Gambling afforded him some semblance of independence and a faint glimmer of glamour.

Whenever he hit a winning streak, he would treat us to fabulous meals at expensive restaurants and sent glasses of dessert brandy to strangers at nearby tables with great flourish. Mama soon learned to go through his pants' pockets as soon as he fell asleep after a late night at the card club. She routinely confiscated his occasional winnings and stashed them away into various hiding places before Papa could squander them on extravagances we could ill afford. She usually forgot where she had hidden the money, and whenever she accidentally discovered some of those emergency funds, they always came as welcome surprises that only forced her to find a new hiding place for them until we really needed them.

Although she once had good reason to trust the long-standing tradition that the male head of the house was responsible for the financial support of his family, once away from Prague, Mama quickly realized she could no longer depend on Papa to provide a stable income. If we were to survive, she knew she herself had to earn money.

Unable to find a job, not only because she did not speak French, but because of draconian laws that prevented non-citizens from obtaining work permits, Mama signed up for classes at *Antoine's*, one of the fanciest beauty services and cosmetics firms in Paris. Soon she persuaded Papa to help her concoct face cream, cologne, and bath oils from recipes she had somehow managed to "smuggle" out. She packaged them into pastel-colored glass containers she had frosted with acid to simulate Lalique crystal, decorated them with pretty ribbons and tiny silk violets, lilacs, or lilies of the valley, and sold them to neighborhood boutiques. She augmented those earnings by hand-sewing satin and lace collars and cuffs for ladies' dresses and suits, embellishing them with beads and embroidery, allowing neighborhood dressmakers to pass them off as their original creations.

My brother Fredo and I were sent away to a small boarding school near Versailles, leaving our parents unencumbered, free to devote themselves exclusively to their various enterprises. At their tiny hotel apartment in the Porte de Saint Cloud *arrondissement* of Paris, Mama cooked on a hot plate set up on the toilet tank and washed dishes and laundry in the bathroom sink. Fredo and I had to take turns visiting them because there was only room for one of us at a time.

My brother and I both hated our school, a small private establishment, which, unknown to our parents, was run by a Communist couple who often took us to party rallies. The most memorable incident during our stay there happened on the fourteenth of July, 1939, when all the students were taken to the *Place de la Bastille* to join a huge crowd waving red flags, clenched fists held high, as we marched around in a circle singing the *Internationale*. Fireworks were exploding all around us, and it all felt very festive and exciting. We did not know that, less than two months later, France would be at war.

On September 1, 1939, World War II broke out. Papa disappeared for two weeks. I did not find out until much later that he guessed this would be no ordinary war and decided he had to find a safe place for us to hide. He smuggled himself into Spain, which had recently survived a terrible, three-year-long civil war won by Fascist dictator Francisco Franco with the help of Hitler and Mussolini. Papa figured that, at least, we would not be bombed or shot at, because Spain was in no position to become involved in another war. However, during his clandestine stay in Spain, the lingering presence of Nazi troops convinced Papa some precautionary measures were in order before we could feel safe there.

"We're moving to Barcelona," he announced on his return. "But before we go, we will be baptized. First we will become Lutherans, then Catholics, so if anyone asks, we can say we used to be Protestants."

Puzzled, I asked: "Why are we doing this?"

"It is not safe now for anyone to be a Jew," Papa explained.

"Are we Jews?" I asked.

Like so many assimilated Jews, my parents had kept that fact from my brother and me to protect us. When could Jews ever feel truly safe? Thus we spent our early childhood years with no knowledge of our roots, without feeling connected to any traditions passed on to us from one generation to the next, deprived of any spiritual grounding. Our parents clearly felt it was more important to keep us safe by hiding from us any knowledge of the constant storm clouds on the horizon that have threatened Jews for centuries.

A romantic, idealistic, eleven-year-old child, full of fantasies inspired by the courage of real-life heroes I had read about, I felt that denying we were Jews was a cowardly lie. Although I did not know what it meant to be a Jew, I felt that it was wrong to deny who we were. I asked to speak to the priest who was to baptize us.

"Joan of Arc refused to deny her voices even though it meant she would be burned at the stake," I reminded the priest. "Papa wants us to lie. I think that's wrong."

He put his arm around me: "Do as your father says," he urged. "Jesus was a Jew. He'll understand." Unconvinced, I was certain that by submitting to baptism, I would lose the right to ever call myself a Jew.

After the brief instructions, followed by rushed baptismal ceremonies, we were once again ready to leave behind everything we owned, including our previous identities. We officially changed our names, and, with new passports, baptismal certificates, French exit and Spanish entrance visas in hand, carrying small, unobtrusive suitcases containing only clothes and photographs, we took a train to the Spanish frontier. Armed with valid-looking documents, following an initially terrifying but finally uneventful border inspection, we proceeded on to Barcelona.

My parents were fortunate to find two furnished rooms for rent in a lovely fifth floor flat owned by a Spanish widow, *Señora* Angela Carron. Mother of a well-known poet who was forced to flee the country after Franco's victorious troops finally entered Barcelona, her personal contribution to the war effort against the Fascists was to pour hot oil on any of Franco's soldiers who was unlucky enough to pass under her balcony.

While Fredo and I attended Barcelona's *Lycée Français*, our parents began to plan how to survive in yet another foreign country, this time one closely allied with Hitler. Despite the presence of machine-gun-toting *Guardias Civil* and army personnel patrolling every part of the city, I remained blissfully unaware of my parents' ever-present fear that we would be found out and sent back to France.

Besides developing a severe case of puppy love for one of the Swiss students at the *Lycée*, Francois Bally, who never guessed my secret crush, I also fell in love with Spain: the architecture, the smells, the music, even the food *Señora* Carron's maid, Pilar managed to scrounge up on the black market and transform into mysterious dishes: Pilar explained that the little rose-colored bags sprouting tentacles covered with minute suction cups swimming in garlicky tomato sauce were baby octopus. I grew to love them and the tiny clam-like barnacle univalves sautéed in spicy olive oil, and its ominous-looking cousin, the goose-neck barnacle, looking like a black-scaled, finger-long snake with a pig-hoof-like head, a delicacy called *percebes*, now offered as an *hors d'oeuvre* in Spain's priciest restaurants.

I first saw this monstrosity placed like a centerpiece on a platter on our table, a medusa-like cluster of finger-sized snakes growing out of a wig of seaweed, watching in horror as each moved a little bit, just enough to confirm it was alive! *Señora* Carron demonstrated how to eat it: you tear one snake finger off the cluster, hold it firmly while giving the hoof-head a twist to detach the skin, and bite off the magenta-colored, raw flesh hanging from the hoof! Neither Mama nor my brother could bear to watch, much less eat it, but Papa and I soon learned to develop a passion for these odd creatures.

Pilar also taught me to speak Spanish as well as *Catalán* and dance the *Sardana* (both banned by Franco as revolutionary), and to cook fish *Catalán* style, sautéed with olive oil and olives, garlic, as well as other delicacies using whatever ingredients she could find. Pilar often took me to church with her on Sundays and holy days. My parents did not object. Exposed to formal religion for the first time, I was enchanted by the pomp and pageantry of Catholic rituals. For someone feeling as guilty as I for lying about my true identity, I eagerly embraced the priests' frequent reminder that "Jesus died for all sinners" and his promise of forgiveness. No one else in my family was as affected either by feelings of guilt or need of redemption as was I.

Having left behind all we owned except our clothes and a small amount of cash when we fled from Paris, Mama once more took over the financial management of our lives soon after we arrived in Barcelona. Without any prior experience, she decided to manufacture gloves. She made left and right hand cardboard patterns using flour and cotton puffs to outline her fingers and produced glove samples with crocheted tops sewed to leather bottoms cut from an old suede coat.

After charming the owner of Barcelona's biggest department store, *Señor Martí-Martí*, into placing an order, Mama confessed she had no money to buy supplies. Touched by her plight and impressed with her plucky know-how, he gave her a letter of credit, instructing his suppliers to provide her with whatever she needed to fill his order.

Mama then enlisted Pilar's help to recruit and train some of her women friends who were grateful for the opportunity to earn extra money at home. She taught them to crochet the glove tops and hand-sew them onto the leather bottoms. By the time we left Barcelona for New York two years later, when thanks to Uncle Milos' intervention, our American entry visas were finally approved, a thriving cottage industry was in operation. Once again, everything we owned remained behind. As soon as we arrived in New York, Mama rented an apartment in a good uptown section of Manhattan, large enough to accommodate several boarders to help pay the rent. During all her years in America, she never felt secure enough to invest in a home of our own. "What if we have to run again?" she would ask.

Mama's ingenuity under pressure, no matter what the circumstances, was prodigious. While Papa floundered, discouraged, lost without his former identity as a productive and respected professional, Mama, unburdened by such pretensions, was doggedly committed to keeping us not only fed and housed, but living with style and beauty, determined to do whatever it took to accomplish that.

Mama's motto was: "If you can put up three hems a day, you'll never starve." While Papa drowned his despair at *Café La Coupole*, where other displaced, middle-aged, male refugees met every afternoon to play cards, complain, and commiserate with each other, Mama kept us financially afloat with her sewing skills. She passed herself off as a seamstress and was hired as an accessories designer at the renowned *Lilly Daché Salon*.

Although she had to leave behind in Prague her beloved collection of Dresden figurines, clear, red, and blue Bohemian cut crystal, and most of her exquisite, hand-made lace trousseau linens, Mama became an expert at finding treasures in thrift shops and at auctions, filling our New York apartment with antique furniture, oil paintings, and oriental carpets, even though two bedrooms at the end of the hall were rented out to strangers.

Everyone at work loved Mama. Her generosity and concern for anyone she felt to be in need was legendary, from bringing lunch every day for a co-worker who could ill afford it, to keeping a pregnant, recent refugee supplied with hand-knitted baby clothes and other essentials. Always eager to improve our financial situation, Mama taught herself bookkeeping and was eventually hired to take over the credit department at a large real estate conglomerate.

She was in her seventies when she became alarmed because her company was downsizing by computerizing every department. Aware how many of her co-workers had already been let go, she was certain she would be next. Unable to contain her anxiety, she confronted her boss: "I don't like surprises," she announced. "Tell me now when you're planning to fire me."

"I wouldn't think of firing you. You can stay here as long as you want," he reassured her. "No machine will ever replace you".

Just in case he changed his mind, she taught herself to use a computer and remained on her job for many more years, long after her boss, determined to hold on to his most dependable employee, paid her in cash under the table so she did not have to declare it. After she finally quit working in her mid-eighties, she began to volunteer at a nearby hospital, tending to the needs of "those old people," running errands, writing letters, and taking care of their bills.

Mama became the most active tenant at a senior citizen residence hotel, to which she moved after being held up at gunpoint twice in the elevator of the apartment building where our family had lived for several decades. Despite a long list of other seniors waiting their turn to move in, Mama persuaded the residence director to admit her immediately.

"If that mugger kills me next time, my death will be on your head," she warned him. It worked. She soon became the residence's star fund-raiser by baking the most delicious cookies, knitting baby items, and recycling others' unwanted gifts to be sold at their yearly bazaar.

Once Mama received a form postcard from her long-time physician, announcing he would no longer serve as her doctor, listing a phone number where his replacement could be reached.

"How dare he do that to me?" she stormed indignantly when she called to tell me about it. "Who does he think I am?"

After a few days she called to give me an update.

"I made an appointment and went to see my doctor. The nurse told me to take off my clothes. I told her: 'What I came for, I can keep on my clothes.' When the doctor called me in, he was sitting behind his desk.

"'The nurse tells me you don't want to take off your clothes,' he said. 'After all this time you're becoming bashful?'

"'No. I am here because I am angry with you,' I told him. 'You have been my doctor for years. How can you just send me a little green card to tell me you can't be my doctor anymore? Do I look like someone you can push away, tell me to go to someone else without asking me first, to find out if it's okay with me, do it with respect, like I'm a *Mensch*?' "

"What did he say?" I asked.

"What do you expect? He apologized and thanked me! And he promised to tell the insurance people who had sent out the card that he wanted to keep me as a patient."

How could anyone help admiring Mama? So, whenever someone told me how lucky I was to have such an amazing mother, I just smiled and said nothing. Who would ever believe that I, her own daughter, could not wait for the time when I was old enough to be on my own and move away to escape her awe-inspiring but joyless, pessimistic influence? No one except my family knew that her sunny, supportive, and generous alter ego was reserved exclusively for her co-workers and any other outsiders.

I was always puzzled and confused by the way Mama could make me feel inadequate and insecure while at the same time inspiring me with her wisdom and expertise about everything. She challenged or dismissed every opinion, each decision I dared to express. She seemed to exert a strange power over me: from my early childhood on, I was convinced her judgments and predictions were infallible. Mine always seemed unreliable at best. I still remember how, whenever she met any of my school friends, Mama would draw me aside, point out one girl and say: "Now, THAT one there is OK, so is THAT one...but watch out for that OTHER one...she'll hurt you."

Of course Mama turned out to be right. It never occurred to me that her warning created in me a mind-set in which trust and friendship could not survive. But, as far as I was concerned, Mama had the uncanny power to see what I was unable to perceive, and, much as I resented her apparent clairvoyance, I nevertheless sought, bought, and depended on her dark vision to guide most of my own decisions. Mama never acknowledged any of my accomplishments or my efforts to please her.

Once, when I was about thirteen, I overheard Mama bragging about my talent as a writer while showing a poem I'd written and forgotten to hide to one of her friends. I burst into the kitchen after her friend left.

"*Muttilein*, you liked my poem!" I exulted.

"That was for HER," Mama corrected. "You and I, we know better."

Only long after I had left home, I found out about *Kinahora*, a Jewish curse whose power Mama clearly feared: she was certain that complimenting any child was bound to bring about some dreadful misfortune to all involved.

Whenever Mama predicted that I was bound to fail at some endeavor, warning me that it was too risky, too expensive, or not worth the effort, more often than not I lost all interest in pursuing it. I cannot begin to guess how many opportunities I missed because I did not trust myself even to try.

Mama was a hard taskmaster, and it was easy to earn her displeasure or dissatisfaction. If I forgot to do one of my chores, or neglected to follow her advice, her punishment of choice was the Silent Treatment. For the smallest transgression, she would inform me, "As your mother, I will of course do my duty: prepare your meals, clean your room, and see to it that you have fresh clothes. But I do not have to talk to you." She then withheld any communication with me, sometimes for weeks at a time.

Once, after enduring twelve days of total silence and her walking past me as though I were invisible, I fell to my knees at her feet, with my arms wrapped around her legs, begging her to look down and talk to me. She ignored my tears and pleas and proceeded to limp away, dragging me along on the floor as though I were a sack of potatoes.

The torture lasted another week. Like me, Papa often became Mama's target for verbal abuse. Again and again, after one of the many times Mama berated him for his shortcomings, she would vent her frustration on me: "You and your father! You're so alike. You'll never get anywhere, and no one will ever love you!"

Nearly every day, when Papa came home, after working at some menial job Mama had finally shamed him into taking, depressed and demoralized by his humiliating lack of status, she would greet him at the door with: "Still got your job?"

Long after I was married with children of my own, Papa, unable to deal with Mama's taunts and derision, would send me long letters describing, in gory detail, why and how he planned to kill himself. No matter where we happened to live, each time I received such a letter, I felt it my responsibility to rush to New

York to defuse what I was certain to be a most critical situation. My supportive presence helped calm Papa, but whatever I said while trying to act as mediator was of course perceived by Mama as a criticism of her.

"You seem to forget that everything I ever did, I did for you," Mama reminded me whenever she felt I did not show her sufficient appreciation. She knew just how to keep me feeling indebted to her forever. I vowed I would never inflict this burden of guilt on any children of my own. Thus I took great pains to assure my son and daughter that, whatever I did, I did it for ME, because doing so gave ME pleasure.

One day, my young daughter angrily confronted me: "How selfish can you be? All my friends have mothers who like doing things for THEM, and you keep reminding me that everything you do is never for me, always only for yourself." I threw up my hands in exasperation. When I tried to explain it all, she replied she still would like to feel that I sometimes did something just for her, because I loved her and loved doing it!

Mama was a magician in the kitchen, but, unlike Pilar, she refused to teach me anything about cooking or allow me access to her kitchen. Once in a while, I got to observe her in action. She made a most unusual cake, not baked in the oven but cooked in a regular pot on top of the stove. I would see her lifting the lid several times, peek at the contents until she finally tipped the pot upside down to spill out the finished confection, complete with chocolate, caramel, or fruit fillings, later served with generous dollops of whipped cream.

Shortly after I was married, I once attempted to impress my husband by baking a cake from scratch. Since no one ever taught me anything about recipes, such as the difference between T.S. (tablespoon) and t.s. (teaspoon), I added double the required baking powder to the batter. When I looked inside the oven and saw the dough rising well above the pan rim, I was certain something was amiss and kept pushing it down. I had also put in the wrong amount of sugar. Fortunately, the pan, which I had placed on my kitchen windowsill to cool, fell out and spilled the cake into the flowerbed below where my husband found me in tears.

"Don't worry," he consoled me after tasting a piece. "It's pretty inedible."

One day, when I was roasting a chicken, a terrible odor filled my kitchen. A neighbor came to ask: "Where are you hiding the decomposing body?" When I told her I had a chicken in the oven, she asked if I had taken out its innards. How was I to know there was a giblet bag tucked deep into the bird's cavity, and that I should have cut open and cleaned out the gizzard before cooking it? Despite such early failings, my love of food eventually drove me to explore ethnic cuisine, and cooking became one of my great passions. Now my twelve-year-old granddaughter and I often putter around in my kitchen, concocting all sorts of dishes.

Mama was also remarkably adept at reworking inexpensive clothes she had bought on sale to look like designer creations just by adding antique buttons, braided belts, and satin or lace details on collars, cuffs, and pockets. Thus sewing, like cooking, a talent Mama guarded jealously as hers alone, became one I later claimed for myself, even hoping in some perverse, wishful thinking, that she would approve, be pleased, even perhaps flattered, because I chose her to be my role model.

While my husband was stationed at Fitzsimmons Army Hospital in Denver, one of my neighbors, who often admired the clothes I sewed for my children, came to me in tears to ask if I could mend the moth holes in her favorite cashmere sweater. I warned her any attempt to mend the holes would show.

"If you let me, I will use the holes as part of a design instead of trying to hide them and create something new," I told her. I transformed her moth-eaten sweater into an elegant garment with strategically placed, jet-bead-trimmed polka dots where the holes had been and lined it in silk chiffon. Somehow the fashion editor of the *Denver Post* heard about my work, interviewed me, and wrote an article illustrated with photographs of the polka-dot sweater, as well as some of my other creations. It all appeared on the front page of the paper's week-end women's section, and suddenly I had a new career: dozens of women called asking if I would work on non-moth-eaten sweaters!

Emboldened by my newfound success, I dared send Mama an elaborately decorated sweater for her birthday. She returned it with a note: "Now that it is no longer mine, I can tell you how you should have done it right."

Even my rare visits to New York usually ended badly, with mutual misunderstandings and hurt feelings. The smallest issue usually escalated into a major confrontation, in which I always ended up the guilty loser. On one such visit, I noticed that none of my children's photos were displayed on Mama's dresser, while those of my brother covered all the available space. I hesitated before bringing up the matter, knowing just how she was likely to respond. When I did, she exploded in anger.

"There you go again! I don't know why you bother to come to New York. You always manage to spoil what little time we have together."

I stormed out and took a short walk to cool off. When I returned, all my children's photos had magically materialized on Mama's dresser top next to my brother's. She never said a word. Neither did I.

I spent years struggling to overcome my self-doubts. Haunted by my long-held conviction that my life was cursed, hearing Mama's words echoing in my ears again and again, confirmed that belief. I did not trust that my husband, or anyone else, could ever love me. During a crucial time in my children's lives, I once again became seriously depressed. When I was unable to cope with my duties, I became a neglectful mother. That is when I decided to seek help and found myself trapped for years in an abusive relationship with Dr. Martin Temple, a highly respected but unscrupulous and manipulative analyst, who used my deepest vulnerabilities, my survivor guilt, and lack of self-esteem, to keep me helpless and dependent on him. I attempted suicide several times, convinced everyone around me would be better off without me.

By the late 1960s, my relationship with my husband, who preferred to devote himself to his professional studies and duties to interacting with the children or me, had deteriorated to the point where there was nothing left to salvage. After twenty-two years of marriage, I decided I did not want to feel at fifty the way I did at forty. The push I needed to act on changing my life came when my husband announced, coming off the podium after receiving his second doctorate: "I think I'll go to medical school."

"I think I'll get a divorce," was my response.

Eventually I quit therapy. Years later, when I had grown strong enough to personally confront the psychologist, I demanded restitution for abuse of trust and malpractice, and emerged victorious and vindicated. But that is another story, to be told later.

With most outer stumbling blocks finally out of the way, I found the courage to test my own strength and connect to my talents, while listening to my own inner voice instead of Mama's. I returned to school, earned a Master's Degree in Psychology, became a licensed Marriage and Family Counselor and Art Therapist, and set up a private practice.

At age sixty, I felt the need to connect to a spiritual part of myself I had neglected too long. I took a break from my clinical work to search for the Jewish roots from which I had been cut off by the Holocaust. After hearing that Fascist Spain had saved the lives of thousands of un-baptized Jews during World War II, I decided to seek out some of those who, unlike my family, had found a safe haven in Spain without abandoning their connection to their Jewish heritage. I also wanted to find some descendants of the medieval *Marranos*, whom I had discovered while at Manhattanville.

Unlike Hitler, who did not make any distinction between Jews who chose to convert and those who clung to their Jewish identities in the face of certain death,

Spanish Jews were given three choices by the Inquisition: convert, leave Spain, or be burned at the stake if they refused either option. Thousands opted for a fourth choice: remain in Spain, submit to baptism, but continue to practice their ancient traditions in secret. Since the time I first found out about the *Marranos*, I felt a deep spiritual kinship with them and hoped that, through a connection to them, I might be able to heal my own lost *Marrana* soul. When Mama found out my search would take me to interview people in Spain and several other foreign countries, she tried to discourage me.

"What about your practice?" she moaned, adding, "You're going to end up a bag lady!"

Once my book was published to good reviews, I heard from others that Mama often bragged about my accomplishments to her friends, stressing how impressed she was with my success. But she never shared her feelings of pride with me. Despite occasional moments of warmth, the fifty-five-year-long, three-thousand-mile, physical separation from my mother only served to remove me geographically from her critical control. Although over time I had built a successful career as a designer, writer, and therapist, and achieved several psychological breakthroughs, distance did not completely neutralize Mama's ability to cut me down with one word by phone or poison most of my rare visits to New York. Eventually our meetings became more problematic and less frequent.

Then, after Mama fell two years ago, breaking some bones, she ended up unable to take care of herself. She found it intolerable to be suddenly helpless and dependent on others at age ninety-five. She announced she had lived long enough and refused to eat or to allow a feeding tube to be inserted. That is how she happened to end up in a hospice.

My brother called me one Friday morning to tell me he did not expect Mama to live through the weekend. I flew to her bedside, certain that this last visit would end like all the others, leaving me angry, sad, overwhelmed with regret and guilt, and with no hope of repair.

What I found at the hospice was a woman transformed. She was alert and animated. Her face seemed soft and looked almost angelic, with her white-blond hair forming a wispy halo around her head. She smiled when she saw me, held my hand as I sat next to her, kissed it repeatedly, and told me all the things I had longed to hear since I was a child. She had apparently abandoned her life-long superstition that to compliment a child would bring down God's wrath: the *Kinahora* curse was gone. She also clearly forgot to be angry. She told me how much she loved me, how beautiful and talented she thought I was, and how proud she had always been of me. I could hardly believe what I was hearing, but I finally accepted she meant what she said after she repeated it again and again.

When I reminded her that I would soon be leaving for Spain again to continue my research, she did not scold me for wasting my time and squandering my money or predict a disaster to discourage me.

"Have a good time," she whispered. "I wish I could go with you."

The day before I left, Mama asked me a question I had heard often during my psychology internship at a hospice many years ago. "What happens when I die?"

I remembered one patient in particular. He had refused to talk to anyone for several days, lying there with his eyes closed. I spent hours just sitting by his bed, softly rubbing his hand to let him know I was there. One day, he opened his eyes and looked at me.

"When I die," he wanted to know, "will there be fire and brimstone?"

"I don't think so," I told him.

"How do you know?" he asked.

I told him about the many patients interviewed by Dr. Elizabeth Kubler-Ross, the famous Swiss psychiatrist and authority on death and dying. Each claimed to have died and "returned from the brink." All told of seeing a bright light on "the other side," at the end of a long tunnel, with loved ones, who had died before, waiting there to welcome them.

"You're sure there is no fire?" he prodded.

"Yes, I am sure."

He smiled, squeezed my hand, took a deep breath, and died. Now here was my own mother, not some stranger, close to death, looking to me for answers.

"What is it like to die?" she wanted to know. "Does it hurt?"

"No, *Muttilein*, it does not hurt," I assured her. "You just get tired and go to sleep. That's all."

"That's all? You're sure?"

"Yes. I'm sure."

She smiled and sighed with relief. I held my breath, afraid she might die right then, but her time had not yet come.

Later that day we reminisced about long-forgotten family get-togethers in Miechenice, a charming mountain village near Prague where we had spent summer holidays for years, before everything changed. At one point Mama's eyes filled with tears.

"I wish I knew if my *Mamichka* has forgiven me for leaving her in Prague. Do you think she knows how hard I tried to get her out?" she asked.

"I'm sure *Oma* Jenny knows and understands," I told her.

"I hope so. I wish I could really be sure."

"Don't worry, *Muttilein*. There is nothing to forgive," I reassured her.

Next day I found it hard to leave. I held her close, hugged her good-bye, told her I loved her, and meant it. We both cried, knowing it was the last time we would see each other. I wept again on the plane, not because I was sad, but out of gratitude for the miracle that happened between us just in the nick of time. A week later, three days after I arrived in Barcelona, my brother called to tell me Mama had peacefully slipped away at the exact moment my plane had lifted off for Spain. She said she wanted to come with me, and she did.

When I arrived back home, I found a brown manila envelope on my bed. I did not know what it was, or how it got there. When I opened it, I saw it was Mama's will, or her "checkout papers," as she called the packet of documents she had sent me long ago.

I remember receiving the envelope back then, and, on peeking into it, seeing it contained a stack of legal papers, I never bothered to examine any of them. I closed the envelope, put it away, and never saw it again until I got back from Spain five years later.

Puzzled, I now spilled out the contents on my bed and saw, among the legal documents, a letter addressed to me, handwritten by Mama. In my hurry to be rid of the papers so long ago, I never noticed the letter. Now that I had found it, I was eager to read it.

Mama addressed me as *Tuttilein*, a diminutive I remember her using when I was a small child. She expressed her love, how proud she had always been of me, and how she hoped I would enjoy the money she planned to leave me. I stared at the letter, wondering how and why I had missed seeing it before. Was there some meaning behind this five-year delay? Why had it mysteriously appeared only after Mama's death?

Then I realized the reason: if I had found and read the letter five years ago, I probably would have torn it up and thrown it away, unable to accept it as anything but a cruel joke, a lie to keep me guilt-ridden forever for feeling about Mama the way I did.

Now, after our last, loving meeting, I was able to read the letter and believe she actually meant every word she wrote. Since then, I often feel Mama hovering nearby, as a comforting supportive presence, and I no longer want to shut her out or run away. I can admit now how much her spirit has inspired me throughout my life, even when I most resented her. I am proud how much of her is part of me.

Again and again I find myself talking to Mama, to tell her about small incidents in my life I know now would give her pleasure. What happened between us during those last few hours together all but wiped away the pain from my memories of her. That's the real miracle. I can at last comfort myself with the hope this was a sign that I have been at least partially forgiven.

5

RECONNECTION

Few of those contemplating therapy are prepared for the way it rips open one's hidden psychic world and leaves one naked and vulnerable before any healing can take place. As far back as I can remember, I have been deeply affected by my dreams, leaving me puzzled, often disturbed by their powerful impact. What did they mean? Were they trying to tell me something, remind me of some forgotten memory I had repressed and needed to remember, warn me of some unseen danger threatening me? Back in the late fifties, I did not know that one could actually learn to decode the subconscious forces creating dreams, to interpret and understand the symbols and images they produced, bring them out into the open, and eventually learn to free oneself of their power.

By 1961, after trying for years to deal with increasingly debilitating survivor guilt and depression, I was finally unable to function, spending days in bed, crying without knowing why. I was thirty-three years old. My children were eleven and nine respectively. I was a successful designer, my husband was working on his second Ph.D. and analytic training, we had a nice home, a circle of good friends, and yet I was obsessed with the wish to die.

After months of resistance, my husband finally convinced me to try therapy. I first met Dr. Martin Temple and his wife when I accompanied my husband to a university faculty event. A stocky man with a shock of graying hair, wearing horn-rimmed glasses and a tweed jacket with leather patches at the elbows, he looked like the typical academic. He was rather shy and soft-spoken and seemed edgy around the other guests. I also noticed he was visibly impatient with small talk.

I knew that Dr. Temple happened to be a practicing Jew. Guessing that my psychic turmoil was most probably caused by the lie that had kept me alive when I should have died with the other murdered Jews, I wondered if a Jewish analyst might perhaps be able to help me. Because I had heard enough disturbing rumors

about psychotherapy, its often addictive, disruptive effect and/or lack of percepti-
ble success, I approached the whole idea of becoming involved in that process
with great skepticism.

"How does it feel to remain a silent observer, while your patients lie on a
couch, revealing their deepest, most intimate secrets to a complete stranger?" I
asked him, startled by the raw mixture of hostility and fear in my voice.

"I do not require that my patients lie on a couch," Martin explained.

"So how does your kind of treatment differ from that more commonly
accepted approach?" I asked.

"My focus is not primarily on sex. I make room for the soul."

That settled it: it sounded safe.

The first few months of our work together were a revelation. Dreams poured
out each night with frightening intensity. Dissecting them disclosed my fears,
longings, and clarified, to some degree, why I experienced myself as a lost soul,
without hope of salvation. They reinforced my conviction that, despite apparent
outer comfort and success, I was destined never to feel at peace or enjoy anything
in my life.

Frightened by the power of the therapeutic process, I embarked on a search for
answers. Determined to make sense out of the earthquake in my psyche, I
devoured book after book dealing with various aspects of psychotherapy. But,
surprisingly, the one book that exerted the deepest personal impact on me,
turned out to be a popular novel, *The Devil's Advocate*, by Australian author Morris West. One of its main characters is a Jewish doctor hiding out in an Italian
mountain village during World War II. He survives by lying about his true identity. Then he finds himself drawn into an inquiry by a priest suffering from terminal cancer, (the title's "devil's advocate") who is sent by the Vatican to
challenge the villagers' claims of miracles allegedly performed by a Communist
guerrilla in their midst. Confirmation of those miracles would be the first step
toward a declaration of sainthood.

Reading about the interaction between these two men triggered a momentous,
emotional breakthrough in my therapy. My identification with the doctor left me
with the first glimmer of hope I could remember. Perhaps some degree of forgiveness might be possible for me after all. I felt compelled to write and thank the
author.

In order for West to understand why his book had such a deep effect on me, I
wanted to give him some background facts about my life as they related to his
characters, especially my guilt over cheating death by hiding my Jewish identity,

and breaking my vow to become a nun. That letter ended up being lengthier than I had intended, but I sent it off anyway.

Shortly after I mailed it to Australia, I read in the *Los Angeles Times* that West was a patient at a local hospital, suffering from terminal cancer, like the priest in his book! I was shocked to read about his illness and immediately sent him a get-well card, wishing him a miracle, adding: "I also sent you a long letter to Australia, but I am certain it will never reach you."

About two weeks later, I was surprised to get a short note from West:

October 12, 1961

Dear Mrs. Alexy,

Your long letter and get-well card reached me in hospital. Many thanks for both of them.

I was deeply touched by your letter and was convinced more than ever that one can never measure the consequences of a simple frank communication of the human dilemma and the human need.

I wish you well and know that you are already arrived in safe harbor.

Sincerely yours,

Morris West.

I kept looking for further updates about his health status, but found nothing. The next news about West did not come until a year later. It was a newspaper article, announcing that he would be signing his most recent book, *Daughter of Silence*, at a local bookstore. Delighted that he had survived, I stood in line with all his other fans the following Sunday, waiting for my turn to get his autograph. When West asked my name, he immediately recognized it:

"You wrote me that long letter!"

He apologized to the others waiting in line, and led me out to a small garden in back of the store. We sat on a bench under a tree and talked for over an hour. He told me that, on the day my card and letter reached him at the hospital, he was told that the X-rays upon which his dire diagnosis was based, actually belonged to another patient!

"You wished me a miracle, and it happened!"

He then proceeded to tell me about himself: A devout Catholic, he had committed himself to life as a monk at the age of fifteen. When World War II broke out, he left the monastery to serve in the Australian army as an intelligence officer. At war's end, he decided not to return to the monastic life, became the *Wunderkind* of Australian radio and television, fell in love, and married.

One day, he suddenly became paralyzed. He spent days out on Sydney Bay on his little boat, fuelled by an iron determination to fight his demons alone, gulping down massive doses of vitamins, too stubborn to submit to therapy. By sheer force of will, he slowly began to regain control over his limbs. While undergoing physical therapy, he fell in love with a nurse who worked with him. Eventually, he left his wife, married the nurse, and had two children.

"Every day since then, I have had to look in the mirror and see a sinner, deal with my guilt over breaking my vows, divorcing, marrying outside the Church. I still consider myself a Catholic, but I carry a heavy burden. That is why I responded so to your story."

Then he added: "Some day I want to incorporate it into a book."

After we said good-bye, promising to stay in touch, he returned to the line of fans waiting for him to sign their books.

We corresponded occasionally during the next year. Then, on June 6, 1962, I received the following letter:

Dear Trudi Alexy,

Ever since you wrote to me, (and your letter is before me at this moment), ever since we met briefly in Brentwood, I have been haunted by your story and by its implications for so many others. I am writing to you now to ask your permission to incorporate it into one of the characters in a new novel.

I could do this without asking your permission since there will be no possibility of identification, and the character, incidents, and setting would be so different that only you would recognize the resemblance. However, you dignified me with a confidence, and a compliment, and I would not like to breach one or feel less worthy of the other.

The new novel, which is highly secret at the moment, is about a bishop who has spent seventeen years in prison under the Soviets, and is finally released. On his return to Rome he finds that he has been made a Cardinal and is later elected Pope: the man who stands between man and God, and who finds between himself and man a vast bureaucracy of the Church.

One of the essential characters will be a woman who, like Catherine of Siena, exercises a singular influence on him and on the life of the Church. I should like to found this character on the story you told me.

As you can see, the theme is way out, and the book will either be the best I have done, or the most resounding failure.

I wonder if you would be kind enough to write me and confirm what I believe will be your consent.

With every good wish to you and your family, and my thanks for what you have given me. Mrs. West joins me in these salutations.

Sincerely yours,

Morris West

That letter reached me during a particularly difficult period of my analysis, which, by then, had taken a most unorthodox turn, causing frightening psychic distortions. One of the issues tormenting me was the pervasive conviction that my deceptions had rendered me un-entitled to anything permanently meaningful or positive in my life. This belief left me with the certainty that nothing good had ever actually happened to me, and that every happy memory was just an illusion. Furthermore, whenever I complained or reached out for anything, a voice in my head screamed: "Shut up, you're supposed to be dead!"

Shortly before I received West's letter, a momentary surge of rebellion prompted me to challenge that debilitating certainty threatening my sanity. I had not had any contact with Nico since 1947. Fifteen years! I once believed our love was the best thing that ever happened to me. Now, it most often appeared as no more than a mirage. Yet, occasional flashes of memory of Nico and everything we experienced together so long ago, appeared to be real, undiminished in intensity. What was I to believe? Was all of it no more than an illusion? Was Nico a mere figment of my imagination?

I had long ago found out that Nico was married. I knew where he lived. I decided to call him.

"Nico, this is Trudi."

My heart was pounding. For what seemed an eternity, he remained silent, as though the name meant nothing to him. Did what I thought we had shared never really happen after all?

Just as I was about to hang up in total despair, he said:

"I'm sorry, but I don't believe I know any Teddy."

"It's Trudi, not Teddy," I shouted.

Now a torrent of words spilled out from him, telling how glad he was to hear my voice, how often he thought about me, how sorry he was that I was already married when he returned from his trip.

"What trip?" I asked.

He then told me that, after meeting with me just once after his return from the Pacific, his parents had refused to give their blessing to his marrying a non-Greek.

"You know how we Greeks are. Just like Jews!"

When he told them he was determined to marry me anyway, they offered a compromise: "Go to Greece for a year. Stay with family. If you both still feel the same by then, we will give you our blessing."

He wrote me from Greece and asked me to wait for him. That letter and several others never reached me. Nico told me he had called Mama twice, and she first told him I was away on vacation.

"She promised to forward my letters to you, but when I received no answer, I grew worried and decided I did not want to wait any longer and flew to New York."

He called Mama as soon as he got to town, to tell her he had come back for me. But Mama told him that I was already married.

"When did you last call Mama? I asked.

"In August, 1947."

"I did not get married until December 1947."

Mama knew that I would never have flown to California to get married if I she had given me Nico's letters or told me that he had called. Nico and I simultaneously realized that Mama's lie had permanently altered the course of both our lives. As we continued to talk, we began to understand that, although so far removed from one another for so long, we had lived through startlingly parallel experiences. Like me, Nico had suffered from overwhelming bouts of suicidal depression and bipolar illness, triggered by the death of his two-year-old son, who was crushed under the wheels of a garbage truck during a moment of distraction, when he was home alone, caring for him.

Although Nico remained close to his three other children and his wife and was still very much involved with his church and huge extended family, it was now clear that he had never forgotten me, or what we had together so long ago. At last I had concrete proof that my experience with him, and our love, had not been an illusion after all.

After more than a tearful hour catching up with each other, we promised to stay in touch. It was just a few days after this phone conversation with Nico that I received West's letter. My emotional and spiritual connection with a writer whom I had only met once, our letters, his using my life story as background for one of the pivotal characters in his new novel, all were proof that here was another meaningful experience, and my memory of it, that proved to be real, not just a mirage. In my response to West, giving him permission to use my story in his book, I wrote him about my recent experience with Nico and the affirming effect his own letter had had on me.

I wrote to West several times after that, curious about the progress of his novel. It came out on June 3, 1963, on the same day Pope John XXIII died. Coincidentally, the first sentence in the book is: "The Pope was dead."

The name of the book is *The Shoes of the Fisherman*. It rose to the national best-seller list, and remained there for many months. The name of the character, for which he used my story, is Ruth Lewin. West also included several of my letters to him, nearly verbatim, in the book. The book was eventually made into a film, with Anthony Quinn playing the Russian Pope. In 1974, in another odd coincidence, just as in West's book, an obscure Cardinal Wojtyla from another Communist country, Poland, was elected Pope.

Nico and I spoke occasionally during the next few years, usually when something momentous or traumatic drew us to connect. Whenever we reached out to one another, it was as though we had never been apart. Eventually, those calls became less and less frequent, but I never let go of the secret dream that, some day, somehow, we would be together.

After spending much of the next thirty years wrestling with my self-imposed judgment and its dire consequences in my life, I think God must have decided I had earned a reprieve. In 1975, after Nico's wife died of cancer, and my husband and I had been divorced for some time, with our children grown and married, Nico once again came looking for me. This time, Mama, still living in the same apartment where Nico had spent many weekends so long ago, gave him my most recent address and phone number. I guess she felt she owed us another chance. We fell in love all over again and remained so for the next thirty years.

And now he is gone.

6

ENTRAPMENT

As sometimes happens at the beginning of therapy, when a small window to the psyche is suddenly pried open, shedding light on what had so long been kept hidden in the dark, things moved very quickly for several months. Everything seemed to make sense and I felt energized, more alive than I could ever remember, even hopeful.

However, soon after I began to feel better, I found myself enmeshed in a spiritual and psychological quagmire. I cannot fully explain when or how it happened, but I gradually found myself projecting on Martin Temple a form of godlike power. Using my survivor guilt and need for forgiveness, he was able to convince me that, like a priest with the power to absolve a sinner, he was nothing less than my direct conduit to God. With subtle implications woven almost imperceptibly into our work, our relationship became, for me, the outward barometer of my soul's salvation status. Lacking sufficient self-confidence to trust my own intuition, judgments and perceptions, I had surrendered control over my life to someone whom I had invested with almost super-human qualities, just as I did with my mother. Martin Temple did nothing to discourage those projections, quite the opposite. The effect was irresistibly seductive, both reassuring and terrifying.

The transition from conventional therapy to something more personal and intimate first began with a gentle and increasingly lingering hug good-bye. It then grew to a gradual addition of time at the end of each appointment, during which Martin began to share some of his own dreams and personal issues with me. Soon as much of his material as mine became part of "our work."

While I felt uneasy about what was happening, it also made me feel special. Besides, wasn't he the professional in charge? Didn't that give me a cause to assume there was a therapeutic reason behind the familiarity?

"You understand, of course, I don't do this with other patients," he assured me. "You and I, we have a lot in common, and I know I can trust you to keep this just between the two of us."

Soon lunches became part of every session, three times a week. While I enjoyed these extended sessions, on another level I began to realize that, what was happening, was at best unorthodox. It certainly was not helping me deal with the issues for which I had originally sought therapy, but, by then, I was too caught up in the process to question Martin's methods and goals. Worst of all, I was not only beginning to fall in love with him, but he actively fostered those feelings as well.

When I voiced my embarrassment and concern, he reassured me. "It is called transference. It shows you are making progress, moving to the most productive phase of therapy." When I grew reluctant to share with him some of the erotic fantasies and dreams that had invaded my sleep, he encouraged me to be as graphic as possible.

"Examining the content of the transference is the most powerful tool in producing therapeutic healing," he urged. "Your dreams are a mirror of your soul."

On November 22, 1963, I was on my way to a session, when I heard that President Kennedy had been assassinated. By the time I arrived at Martin's office, I was sobbing. He consoled me, held me, and, in the heat of passion, generated by such sudden physical closeness and long repressed sexual tension, we ended up crossing the line that irretrievably separates the professional realm from the personal. To help me struggle through the resulting shock and confusion, Martin convinced me not to be upset, assuring me that what happened was "a natural and positive transition within the therapeutic process." Once that physical barrier was torn down, acting out our sexual fantasies became a regular part of "our work".

Sex was frequently violent, but I had never before felt so intoxicatingly aroused, so completely satisfied before. The passion I had been too terrified to release with Nico so long ago, and never came close to with my husband, was finally unleashed. While the emotional churning, the ups and downs, the excitement and terror of feeling both special and not special enough, made me feel perversely alive, wanting the agony and ecstasy of it to go on forever, another part of me warned me to run for my life.

One of the major complicating factors was that, because Martin and my husband were professional colleagues, our families were sometimes brought together for various social events. On some level, I knew these outside contacts were not only therapeutically reckless but also unethical. They also proved to be deeply disturbing. Watching Martin interacting with his wife, seeing their affection for each other and their children while having to hide my true feelings and act as though nothing special was going on between us, was agony. Wracked by the realization that, once more, I was living a lie, I was determined to use those emotionally brutal encounters to counteract my ever more frequent fantasies of having a legitimate, open life with Martin, with neither a wife nor a husband in the way, without having to sneak around and pretend.

Eventually my conflict became unbearable. I could not focus on my duties as a mother, or the running of my home. My husband was too engrossed in his studies to suspect anything and only marginally noticed my precipitous re-descent into depression. All I wanted to do was sleep and shut out everything that was tearing me apart: condemnation, disgust, anger, desire, jealousy, terror, guilt and confusion.

Worst of all, whenever I told Martin I wanted to quit therapy, because I was no longer able to cope with the turmoil, he somehow managed to talk me out of it by emphasizing the benefit of hanging in, "toughing it out," overcoming my dilemma by "containing the conflict." He kept reminding me that my spiritual healing depended on how well we managed to work through our relationship. "We'll walk through the fire together," he assured me. I ended up convinced there was no way out, certain there was no one I could turn to who might help me. I felt hopelessly trapped in a vat of glue.

I tried twice to escape by swallowing an overdose of pills, but failed to take enough to cause more than a long, sick sleep. I told no one. Especially not Martin. One day I decided to make one last try. I saved up enough pills to do the job right and took off, driving towards the mountains, planning to go to a motel and escape my agony once and for all. On the way, I kept wrestling with my decision, wondering if I was taking the coward's way out, but ended up convinced that I was no good to anyone anyway, especially my children, and that everyone would be better off without me.

As I approached one of the mountain passes, I noticed a small Spanish-style church on the side of the road. Seeing it brought back all the old feelings I had experienced while attending mass in the chapel of my childhood convent school: the security and peace filling me as I knelt at the altar rail, waiting for Father Hannigan, Marycliff's chaplain, to place the sacred host on my tongue, remembering what it was like to believe God himself was inside me, assuring me of his forgiveness.

Nostalgia and longing overwhelmed me and I began to cry. Unable to continue driving, I parked the car in front of the church and tried to enter the sanctuary. The door was locked. A small cottage set back behind the church appeared to be the rectory. The front door had a shuttered, square opening at eye-level, with a metal mesh grill covering it. I rang the bell. The peep-window squeaked open, and a bearded monk's face appeared in the darkness behind the grill.

"I need help," I whispered.

"What seems to be the trouble?" he asked in a deep Irish brogue.

"I came here to kill myself, but I am afraid to do it. Can you talk to me, please?"

Silence. Then I could see him turning around and whispering something to someone hidden in the shadows.

"I am sorry," he finally said…"I am alone here. I'm not allowed to speak to a woman without someone else being present. You understand, I am a priest. Please come back tomorrow."

The small door behind the grill squeaked shut.

I stopped at the first motel I came to, paid for one night, locked the door of my room, lay down on the bed, and gulped down the whole bottle of pills with a glass of water, and waited to die. Instead, I began to throw up.

"This is not working," I realized, crying, frustrated and afraid. "What if I become a vegetable? The pills might permanently damage my brain instead of killing me!" I called Martin to tell him where I was, and what I had done. He raced to my motel and took me to the closest emergency hospital, to get my stomach pumped.

"What were you thinking?" he asked, once I was out of danger. "How does it me make me look, to have a patient commit suicide? Next time, call me before you do something so stupid!" Then he added: "Don't you know how important you are to me?"

At first I was ashamed that I had failed once more to break away, but soon things went right back to where we had left off, and continued as though nothing had happened. The suicide attempt was never mentioned again, but my depression grew worse. It was during this time that Uncle Milos came to my rescue, and made it possible for me to return to Spain.

7

BREAKTHROUGH

Despite my initial assumption that I had gained new insights and developed a measure of strength during my trip to Spain, it did not take long for me to realize that nothing had really changed, permanently. Returning to the same circumstances, the same environment, made it difficult to hold on to whatever gains I had briefly enjoyed.

A year after my return from Spain, Martin told me that he and his wife were planning to go to Europe for a month. By now my dependency on him had become even more obsessive. My instant reaction was panic. How would I manage without him?

He tried to reassure me. "I promise I will stay in touch," he said, "but, remember, it will be hard to do, with my wife right there. And what would happen if your husband found my letters?"

As I struggled to come to terms with Martin's absence, it suddenly occurred to me that this might be the perfect time for me to finally break away for good. Maybe I would not have to kill myself to escape after all. To make sure he would not be able to contact me, I planned to convince my husband to take the four of us on a family vacation while Martin was gone. He and his wife were due to fly to Paris on Wednesday August 11, 1965, while I planned for my family and I to start driving south, towards Mexico, that same afternoon. However, the morning of their departure, Martin called to tell me the person who had promised to drive him and his wife to the airport was unable to take them, and asked if I could do it.

Feeling that, because we were planning to drive, we could be flexible and leave later than originally planned, I agreed to do it. I convinced myself it would be good for me to actually see Martin leave with his wife, thus concretely reinforcing my decision to break his control over me. I felt as though I were in a trance all the way to the airport. On our arrival, we were informed the plane's departure would be two hours late.

Good. I decided to just drop them off and leave.

"Don't go. Let's all just have few drinks to make the time go faster," Martin suggested.

I seldom drink, but that day I had three Bloody Marys. The time dragged on interminably, and I grew more and more upset. I knew I had to get away before I made a fool of myself, lost control, and blurted out something I was sure to regret.

"I better get going, before I am too drunk to drive," I announced, getting up. "You two have a good trip."

Before either of them could say anything, I made a quick exit, wobbly on my feet, as I half-stumbled, half-ran across the big parking lot to my car, unaware that I was crying, with the mid-day summer sun burning my bare shoulders.

I was trying to get my key into the lock when Martin caught up with me.

"Whoa, wait a minute," he mumbled. "You didn't think I was going to let you go without a good-bye kiss, did you?"

He was smiling, his words were slurred, and he wasn't any steadier on his feet than I was on mine. I was furious. Here he was undermining my resolve again, trying to sabotage my intention to make a clean getaway!

"I won't be here when you get back," I hissed, leaning back against my hot car door to steady myself.

He looked at me a long time, and must have seen something in my eyes that showed him that I meant what I said, because he now came close, pressed his pelvis against mine, rotated it back and forth as the bulge rubbing me hardened. He reached into my silk camisole, and fondled my left nipple until it grew erect. He kissed me hard on the mouth, reeking of liquor, and walked away a few steps. Then he turned around with a smirk on his bloated face:

"Yes, you will. You will be right here, waiting for me, when I get back."

I still don't know how I made it home. On the way, I heard sirens wailing from a distance. When I got into my house, no one was home. I turned on the TV, and there was Watts erupting in a riot of violence and arson. I watched black men torching their own homes and businesses, black kids looting shops owned by their own people, a frenzy of destruction, fueled by years of despair, of being ignored, humiliated, hopeless, powerless to escape their ghetto—till now their only way out was to destroy their own prison—and themselves. I knew exactly how they felt. I understood their despair, their feelings of defeat, I knew what was driving their rage, and I wished I could join them in their revolt.

I decided I would not go to Mexico. When my husband got home, the van he had rented to make our trip more comfortable was all gassed up, and the portable refrigerator was filled with drinks and snacks. He found me staring at the TV screen.

"It's a good thing we're getting out of L.A.," he said, "God only knows how bad this will get. We'd better hurry."

"I'm not going with you," I announced. "You and the kids go. I need some time alone. If I feel better in a day or so, I'll catch up with you."

Our children pleaded with me to come along, but my husband could see my mind was made up.

"It's okay," he told them. "All mommies need a little vacation from everybody once in a while."

"You're sure?" he asked before the kids kissed me good-bye.

I nodded, watched them drive off, and locked the door after them.

I went back to the riots on TV for another few minutes and burst into uncontrollable sobs when I saw two black bodies lying in the street. Young kids, kids who had chosen to die, who preferred death to their unbearable status quo.

How I wished I could go to Watts and die with them!

I eventually fell asleep on the living room couch, and had the following dream:

> *I am walking down a deserted street in Watts, smoking ruins all around me, eerie sounds of sirens and explosions in the distance. I look up at a window in a decrepit old building and see threadbare curtains pull shut as my eyes fix on it. Suddenly I am aware that I am being followed. I turn and see a group of about six or seven black youths walking behind me, sweaty bandanas tied to their foreheads, wearing torn jeans and soiled t-shirts, armed with all kinds of weapons and sticks. As they approach, I hear them talking.*
>
> *"What's a white chick doin' here?" one of them asks as they start to surround me. "Let's give her a taste of what livin' in the 'hood's like."*
>
> *Part of me wants to run away, but I turn around.*
>
> *"I'm sorry about what's happening here, and want to join you in your struggle."*
>
> *They slap their thighs and roar with laughter.*
>
> *"You hear whitey! Whitey say she sorry!"*
>
> *"Wait, you don't understand! I want you to stop killing each other, burning your homes and businesses. Take me instead. Do what you want with me. Let me make up for all the wrongs white people have done to you…"*
>
> *More laughter. Then a moment of silence.*

"Okay! Let's have some fun wid whitey first, and then let's blow her away," one of them now sneers. "Bet she never had her a real homeboy gang-bang!"

Now the youngest of the group, a mere boy, speaks up.

"Spike, I never had me a white chick. Let me have her first. Then you all go at her."

The apparent leader, a skinny kid with his arms covered with tattoos, and a still fresh slash across his left cheek, barks an order.

"Okay, so you go first. You got till mornin' wid her…here, in back of Tom's garage. Have fun! We be back early."

The young boy grabs me, pulls up the corrugated, roll-up door closing off the gas station repair shop, drags me in and pulls it all the way down behind him.

"You scared?" he asks. He looks no older than about fifteen, gangly and grungy.

He grabs a filthy towel and throws it on the floor.

"Get down," he commands.

"Are you going to hurt me now?" I ask.

"What you really doin' here?" he asks.

"I'm looking for someone to kill me. I've tried to do it myself, but I keep messing up. Will you do it?"

The boy looks surprised.

"Why you want die? You white, you got it easy, you don' got to live like us. Us got nothin', no future, no hope. Why you?"

He sits down next to me, and I tell him my story. He tells me his: abandoned by his mother, abused by his father, kicked out of school, drugs, violence. I reach out to him. He leans on my chest, sobbing.

"Ah ain't gonna hurt you," he finally says. "Ah cain't."

He promises to protect me when the others come for us next morning. We curl up with his head on my chest. I take out my left breast.

"Go ahead, take it," I tell him.

He falls asleep suckling on my breast like a baby.

I am awakened when I hear footsteps outside the garage door next morning. I look around. The boy is gone.

I woke curled up on the sofa, sobbing. The TV showed Watts was still burning. I turned it off, went into the bathroom, locked the door, and searched for my husband's double-edged razor. I took out the blade, stood facing the mirror, and cut deep first into one wrist, then the other, watching the blood spurt into the sink.

I was surprised to feel nothing. No pain. No panic. Only an overwhelming sense of relief, of peace.

After a few minutes I began to feel dizzy and looked into the mirror to see my face turn ashen. When I started to feel faint, I tried to hold on to the sink, but slowly slumped to the floor.

I awakened to hear my daughter screaming at me. "Mom, Mom, what did you do? Wake up! Please wake up. Please don't die!"

I opened my eyes. Was I dreaming? Blood was all over me and on the floor, and my child was rocking me back and forth in her arms. There was a splintered hole in the bathroom door, where the lock used to be, and I could faintly hear my husband calling an ambulance. When the paramedics arrived, my son stood, silent, a bewildered, accusing look in his eyes. When he tried to help them lift me onto the gurney, they pushed him aside.

"Get out of the way! No kids here."

"I forgot my camera. Dad let me come back to get it," my daughter explained later, in the lobby of the hospital emergency room. I was lying on a stretcher, conscious, but just barely. My wrists were bandaged tight, but blood kept seeping through the gauze.

My husband stood leaning against a wall and kept looking at me with accusing eyes.

"Did you even consider what it would have been like to find you in a month if...?" His voice trailed off, but he could not conceal his anger. He turned away.

"I don't understand why it is taking them so long to take care of her," he mumbled to himself. He finally walked over to the reception desk. The operator ignored him and kept answering the incessantly ringing phones. One hour. Another. Ambulance attendants kept bringing in other patients on stretchers, bleeding from wounds or moaning with severe burns, rushing past us. They were quickly dispatched to somewhere down the hall.

Finally my husband stopped one of the doctors.

"We've been here for a long time. My wife cut her wrists. She is bleeding. Could you please help her?"

The doctor, his gown streaked with blood, glared at him:

"Listen here. L.A. hospitals are filled with wounded. These were rushed here all the way from Watts. THEY want to live. Your wife doesn't. Let her wait."

Much later, a nurse finally wheeled me back to the end of the corridor. Without giving me anything to dull the pain, she removed my bandages and proceeded to sew up my cuts with what felt like a very blunt needle.

"You can remove the stitches in a week," she said, "if the cuts don't get infected." She left, my husband wheeled me out, lifted me into our car, and drove the children and me home. My daughter slept with me in my bed that night. Neither of us spoke, but the look of fear and anger in her eyes haunts me to this day. Two days later, we all took off for Mexico, with me wearing a long sleeved shirt to hide my bandaged wrists.

Seven days later, before anyone was awake, I shut myself into the large, ornately tiled bathroom of our suite in the Colonial Inn in Morelia, sat on the toilet, and, using a pair of tiny nail scissors and tweezers, cut the black sutures in my wrists and pulled them out. On my return, Martin did not challenge my story when I explained I had accidentally fallen through a glass door, and asked how I enjoyed Mexico. The "accident" was never mentioned again. Neither was the incident at the airport.

Soon it was business as usual again.

8

A GLIMMER of HOPE

By the time we returned from Mexico, my wrist wounds had healed pretty well, although they still looked raw. But, physically as well as emotionally, I felt defeated and hopeless as I once again found myself sinking into quicksand. As though sleepwalking through a nightmare, I returned to my old routine. About this time, Martin began asking me to read and critique some of his recent theoretical writings, and, although I resented the burden, I was afraid to refuse. I found the writing stiff and pompous. The more I got involved reading and making editing notes in the margins, the more it occurred to me that perhaps I myself should try to write. I even dared think I might do better than Martin!

I had kept a diary for years, though not recently, and remembered relishing the privacy and freedom in pouring my thoughts and feelings onto paper. I soon joined a writing class at a nearby junior college. As we read aloud some of our work, taking turns critiquing, suggesting, and encouraging each other, I was exposed, for the first time, to the camaraderie and intimacy engendered by opening up, and sharing my creative efforts with the others. It all had an enormously liberating effect on me. I was still not ready to fully reveal the most private facts of my life, but I learned to express parts of my inner truth by fictionalizing it. Some of the friendships, formed during that period, remain part of my life to this day.

My first writing attempt was an article in the form of a letter from a mother to her young daughter, discussing the mystery of her new sexual awakenings. I was encouraged by my instructor to submit the article to a contest run by *Writer's Digest* and won an honorable mention. The prize: a volume of the current *Writer's Markets*, full of useful guidelines and helpful suggestions as well as effective ways to market one's work.

Thus emboldened, I now threw myself into more serious writing. I tackled what eventually turned into a short novella called *The Octopus*. The protagonist,

Rachel, is a young girl, whose family is forced to flee France, just as the Nazi roundup of Jews begins in 1940. Rachel, her brother and father manage to escape to Spain, after her mother is brutally killed in front of Rachel's eyes, rendering her so frozen with fear that she cannot do anything to stop it. She is also unable to bring herself to say good-bye to her best friend, Miriam, who is too ill with leukemia to escape with her family. The essence of the story is how Rachel deals with her survivor guilt, and how intervening in the barbaric ritual killing of a baby octopus, in a tiny Spanish fishing village, brings about self-forgiveness and ultimate redemption.

Writing became my safe haven. Everything else in my life seemed to recede into the background, although the daily routine remained the same. All that mattered was the act of shifting my attention from my outer reality to the inner, creative one. It magically transformed the way I related to everything around me: writing made my life bearable.

I instinctively knew not to share any of my work with Martin, certain he would find ways to be critical and discourage my efforts. After all, I had dared to intrude on his territory. In the midst of this period of exhilarating creative productivity, a friend asked if I might be willing to translate a German article about his friend, the writer, Henry Miller, which had recently appeared in the periodical *Der Spiegel*. It was a pseudo-psychological dissection of Miller's sexual and moral attitudes, as expressed in his writings.

I agreed to do the translation. I was familiar with most of Miller's work and considered my mother tongue, German, though somewhat rusty due to non-use, still adequate. However, I did not expect to have to rely on a German-English dictionary as often as the article's typically convoluted, multi-syllabic German syntax required. One of the phrases that stumped me was, of all things, the title of one of Miller's books. Could this be one I had never heard of? In referring to the dictionary I came up with *The Radius of the Ibix*.

When I finally figured out that the title referred to *The Tropic of Capricorn*, I dissolved into laughter.

"You must tell Henry this story," said my friend. "It'll give him a good chuckle."

A week later, he invited me to a party at which Miller was a guest. "Bring your translation."

When I told Miller my story, he roared. We spent much of the evening talking. In his late seventies by then, he was amazingly youthful and energetic, with slits for eyes and a baldpate that made him look like a skinny Chinese guru. He was curious and opinionated about a myriad of subjects, from politics to the theater, from sexual repression to the influence of other contemporary writers. Besides his passion for watercolor painting, (his book, *To Paint is to Love*, had recently been published), he mentioned he was taking piano lessons from famed pianist, Jacob Gimpel, who happened to have been my Uncle Milos' boyhood friend! Gimpel and Milos had been fellow piano students both in Europe and later with Rosina Levine in the U.S.!

What impressed me most about Miller was his gentle self-deprecating sense of humor, and the way he quickly put me completely at ease. When he asked what he could do to thank me for doing the translation, I had the nerve to ask for one of his acclaimed watercolor paintings, and he agreed to give me one! During the course of the evening, I mentioned my recent efforts at writing. True to his reputation as a champion of struggling writers, he immediately expressed interest and said he hoped I would visit him soon.

Two days later I received the following letter from Miller, dated May 30, 1966, with the envelope addressed to my name, and below it, in caps, WRITER!

Dear Mrs. Alexy,

The moment I got home last night I read your translation of Von Eugen Skasa-Weitz's article. I don't doubt you had trouble translating it! His text sounds very much like I thought when I skimmed through it in the original. Somehow I cannot help thinking of him (or her?) as a sort of fatuous jackass, the kind of German pundit who has to complicate even the simplest thoughts and who, in the end, really says nothing. I am sorry you had to waste your good time on it.

I get letters from very young people, even in Germany, who can give me better interpretations of my work than this learned individual. It seems to me he is like a horse with blinders who knows only one road, and that is—back to the stable. The stable in this case is the psychoanalytical nest in which he saw the light of day.

Forgive me if I seem too harsh in my criticism. I am reminded of a wonderful interview I read just recently in Mc Call's magazine, (May issue) an interview with Pablo Casals [the world-famous Spanish cellist], in which he says he learned nothing from the great philosophers, that, indeed, he learned more, much more, from a simple fisherman he once met. (much like Siddhartha and his encounter with the old ferryman, remember?)

I shan't forget to send you a watercolor, and it will be a great pleasure to do so. I enjoyed so much talking to you last night.

Sincerely

Henry Miller

This was but one of several letters Miller sent to me, on a variety of subjects. He also occasionally mailed me invitations to events he thought I might enjoy. Among his missives was a photo postcard of himself as an adorable three-and-a-half-year-old, dressed like a little dandy, in a frilly white shirt under a velvet jacket, and matching knickers, a huge bow at the neck, black patent leather shoes, and an odd-shaped, large hat, sporting a white feather! It is autographed, and the inscription on the back reads:

Thought you might put this next to a mezuzah, if you have one. Will bring good luck! HM

This, thirty years before I published my first book, *The Mezuzah in the Madonna's Foot*!!!

A week after we met, Miller called, to invite me to visit him at his Pacific Palisades home.

"Bring your story," he ordered.

When I arrived, manuscript in hand, a housekeeper let me into the foyer and disappeared. Looking through the large living room, past the wall of sliding glass doors, to the patio beyond, I could see Miller and a young girl engaged in an energetic game of ping-pong. Both were nearly naked, except for his jock strap and her barest of bikini panties!

I stood transfixed for a few minutes, and then approached the patio. Miller eventually caught sight of me, smiled and waved. "I'll be right in," he shouted. "Make yourself comfortable."

When he and the girl finally joined me, both were covered with strategically draped towels.

"Say hello to Linda," he said. "She's my ping-pong buddy."

He kissed Linda good-bye. She left and Miller put on a robe.

"Let's go to my office," he suggested, leading the way.

It was small, cluttered, with books scattered everywhere around his desk. One white wall was completely covered with brief messages, signed by dozens of guests who had visited him. Some were unknown to me, but most belonged to well-known writers, artists, and other cultural icons.

"That's my guest book. Go ahead, sign it."

I can't remember what I wrote, besides my name, I was so awed at the thought of adding my autograph to that illustrious list.

Miller sat down behind the desk.

"So, let me see what you brought."

I had expected to drop off the forty pages of *The Octopus*, for him to read at leisure, but he seemed eager to tackle it then and there.

"Why don't you look around, while I read. Go! You're welcome to browse anywhere."

I tried to protest, but Miller insisted. "No, no, I read fast, and then we can discuss what you wrote."

While I took my time looking at the jumble of fascinating books, manuscripts, drawings, watercolor paintings, maps, and photographs of Miller, with other easily recognizable celebrities, I tried hard to displace my anxiety with the excitement of having someone of his renown actually offering to read and discuss my amateurish writing effort.

He seemed to take forever. By the time he finally called me, and asked me to sit next to him, I was trembling.

"You can write," he began, "but this is not my cup of tea."

My heart plummeted.

"You said you are familiar with my work," he continued. "So you must know that, for me, what I know, what I see, and what I experience, is all I care to write or read about. People, how they interact with each other, what they feel, what affects them and why—that has always been what interests me."

Miller saw my crestfallen face and reached over and touched my hand.

"Don't be discouraged, Trudi. You write well. But your style is more like Anais'. You know her work, don't you? Sort of mystical, allegorical, even spiritual. She also lived in Barcelona as a child, and her father was a Spaniard. So you have a lot in common. She will be a better judge of your work. I want you to meet her. I will send her *The Octopus*."

Anais Nin. Of course I knew her work. Although the first volume of her scandalous *Diary* had just been published, I had not yet read it, but rumors about its provocative content had preceded it. I had read some of her dream-like novels, knew about her daring love affairs, her years as Miller's muse and lover in France, and was aware that it was Nin who was ultimately responsible for launching

Miller's writing career by arranging for the publication of his first book, *Tropic of Cancer*, long banned in the U.S.

I agreed to leave *The Octopus* with Miller and, after I thanked him for offering to introduce me to Nin, we spent another hour in conversation. When we first met at our mutual friend's home, he had spent much of the time asking questions about my life. This time, he spoke mostly about himself, sharing rather intimate details of his current love affair with a young Japanese lounge singer, Hoki Tokuda, and his frustration because her ever-present "chaperone" did not allow them to have private time together! (Hoki, who was more than fifty years his junior, eventually became Miller's fifth wife).

Many saw Miller as "a foolish old man who allowed an unscrupulous and ambitious floozy to take him for a cruel ride." But all this happened much later. At this moment, he acted like a besotted, teen-aged lover in agony.

I felt a surge of compassion for this sentimental old man who wore his bleeding heart so shamelessly displayed on his sleeve and reached over to give him a hug. Major mistake! He immediately began kissing me on the mouth. I somehow extricated myself as gently as I could. For a moment, there was an awkward silence.

"I could not resist," he finally said. "You are quite a dish."

Though flattered, I was mostly aware of Miller's bad breath.

When I was finally ready to leave, the watercolor I hoped to take with me was forgotten. Miller promised to set up a meeting with Anais Nin.

We shook hands, but when he opened the front door to let me out, he stopped me.

"I see you drive," he said, looking at my car in the driveway. "I don't. I ride a bike. I want to make you an offer. I love French films, and it is hard for me to get to see them. If you will agree to occasionally take me to see one, I'll take you to dinner afterwards. How about it?"

How could I resist such a tempting offer? What an opportunity to spend time and pick the brains of a famous author!

During the course of the next two years, he asked me to take him to see more than two dozen French movies. He always dressed casually chic when I picked him up, in matching khaki shirt and pants, topped off with a roguish tweed visor cap and jacket. He often held my hand in the dark theater, whispering wistfully: "No one knows to make romantic films like the French!"

Afterwards he would suggest I drive him to one of his favorite Hollywood hangouts, either Cock'n Bull, or Villa Frascati (long gone now) for a late dinner, where everybody seemed to know him. As they greeted him, they unabashedly looked me over, probably wondering who Miller's new chick might be. I loved that he introduced me as "my friend and fellow writer, Trudi" and am a bit embarrassed to admit I thoroughly enjoyed those few moments of notoriety by association.

Dinner always began with often delicious, juicy gossip about some of the people seated all around us. This was followed by a fascinating discussion of the film we had just seen, and I was surprised and pleased that he seemed just as interested in my opinions as expressing his own. I was amazed at his passion, keen sensitivity, and psychological insight into the situations and relationships portrayed on the screen.

One day, I received an invitation to an afternoon event in the famed Bradbury Building in downtown Los Angeles, honoring Anais Nin. The invitation had been addressed to Miller, but he had substituted my name and address. "I won't be able to go, so take advantage of this occasion to meet Anais," he wrote. "I've already told her about you and sent her *The Octopus.*

I had never been inside the Bradbury building, one of Los Angeles' most honored architectural treasures. Nothing about its exterior gave a clue to the magic that greeted me inside. First, I saw a rather long, narrow atrium, covered by a glass dome, flooding the interior with natural light. Everywhere I looked I saw, on both sides of this atrium, a profusion of exquisite wrought-iron latticework rising to the dome. Wrapped around each of the exposed floor levels, the intricately fashioned railings were vaguely reminiscent of New Orleans French Quarter balconies. Ornate elevators were enclosed inside cages, resembling tall filigree towers. Facing me was a set of oddly asymmetrical stairs that rose to the top. Every view brought to mind antique lace. A large crowd was milling around, and, at first, I was so overwhelmed by the beauty surrounding me, I did not rush to look for Anais Nin. I finally found her holding court on one of the upper levels, a cluster of admirers crowding around her.

The first thing that struck me about her was her strawberry blond beehive of hair, parted in the middle, above an inordinately high forehead. Her large, almond-shaped eyes were heavily outlined with kohl, and her flawless pale skin had the quality of peach-colored matte satin. When I finally got closer, I noticed her feet: tiny, they were shod in delicate, low-heeled, strappy sandals of metallic copper that perfectly matched her hair, and the variegated pastel watercolor-wash, floral print of her diaphanous silk chiffon gown. The total effect was to give her an otherworldly ethereal aura.

She spoke so softly, I could not hear a word, but I stood transfixed, watching the graceful way she used her delicate hands, animated like birds in flight, to emphasize whatever she was saying, holding her audience in thrall. I waited until the crowd thinned out a bit and approached her.

"I am Trudi Alexy. I believe Henry Miller…"

"Of course!" she interrupted with slightly French-accented, breathy words. "I just read your *Octopus,* and I'd love to talk to you about it, but not here. It's too noisy and not enough private. Could you come to my home? I live in Silver Lake. Please call me."

Assuming I would know how to reach her, she turned to attend to another group of admirers waiting to speak with her. When I called her next day, she gave me directions and invited me for tea the following afternoon. Nin's home, overlooking Silver Lake, was built by Eric Wright, Frank Lloyd Wright's son, and is most reminiscent of his father's style: organic, elegant, and simple. It has a Japanese garden and a pool, where Nin swam daily. Eric's half-brother, Rupert Pole (his mother was married to another Wright son, Lloyd, also an architect) commissioned the home in 1961, as a love-gift for Nin, whom he married in 1947.

When Pole and Nin met and married, she was forty-four years old and he was half her age. Ultimately, their marriage had to be annulled, when it was revealed that Nin's legitimate husband, Hugo Guiler, to whom she had been married (but never divorced) since 1923, was alive and well in New York. Legally married or not, Pole remained Nin's most faithful lover for thirty years, until her death in 1977.

Nin greeted me warmly, wearing a simple, loose kimono, in subtle shades of lilac and lime, and offered to take me on a tour of her home. The interior had a Japanese ambience. What struck me most were the many stunning, framed collages constructed by Nin's artist friend, Jan Varda, using exquisite shiny and rough silk cuttings in various shapes, sizes and surprising color combinations. The simple furnishings seemed chosen to coordinate with the collages. Then she invited me to sit on green and purple striped silk pillows, next to a low table set with rust colored dessert dishes, a terrine full of tiny fruit tortes and nuts, and a Raku teapot filled with a fragrant Japanese brew.

She began by asking me to tell her about my life, in order to understand how it influenced the plot of my novella. "Your *Octopus* would make a lovely film," she finally said. "Henry was right. This is very much my kind of story. I have a wonderful screenwriter now working on one of my novels, *The Spy in the House of Love.* I will talk to her and will give you her phone number. Be sure to call her."

I cannot remember what else happened, or what we discussed. All I recall was that I felt bewitched by this nymph-like creature, who moved with the grace of a dancer, and spoke in a breathless whisper like a haunted child. Before I left, she gave me a copy of the just-published first volume of her *Diary*, and inscribed it: "Anxiously awaiting your first book. Keep on writing! Anaïs Nin." I never saw her again. I also never contacted the writer she wanted me to meet. I lent my treasured copy of my autographed *Diary* to a friend whose house was destroyed in a fire that reduced everything in it to ashes, including Nin's book.

Years later, I happened to have dinner with a friend, Bob Goldfarb, who was, and still is, an agent for film writers. I had just returned from another trip to Spain, and told him about an upsetting incident I witnessed While shopping in a store, I had overheard a group of German tourists loudly ridiculing Spaniards in a most insulting and chauvinistic manner. Much as I wanted to confront them, tell them I understood German, and was appalled by their behavior, I remained silent, paralyzed, and left the store, filled with shame. I then told Bob about *The Octopus* and added "I reacted just like Rachel, when her mother was being murdered!"

"That's an interesting coincidence," he replied, and told me that he had recently become involved in a film project, based on a story that had appeared some time ago in the *New Yorker*.

"It deals with a similarly upsetting incident in Italy, called *At Lake Lugano*. One of my clients is due to write the screenplay, and I plan to produce it."

Bob happened to have a copy of the *New Yorker* in his briefcase and offered to let me read the article. "I am excited that you have started to write!" he added. "You must let me read *The Octopus*."

Next time we met, I returned the *New Yorker* and gave him a copy of my novella. Two days later Bob called me to tell me he had given *The Octopus* to his screenwriter client. She read it, thought it would make a great film, and asked to meet me! The screenwriter turned out to be Barbara Turner, the same one Anaïs Nin had asked me to call so many years before!

A few days later, Bob gave a small dinner party, and invited both of us. Barbara and I talked at length that night, and with her sharp intuition, she guessed that I was trying to work through events in my childhood that were still deeply affecting and influencing my life. I ended up telling her about my despairing "Watts" dream and subsequent suicide attempt.

"You must write this," she urged. "*The Octopus* is merely an introduction to the real story. If you won't write it, I will."

Although Barbara and I have kept peripherally in touch since then, we never worked together. Eventually she became too busy to take on anything on spec, too involved with other projects, and earned well-deserved renown for writing such films as *Petulia, Georgia, Pollock* and *Company*. Her style is so distinctive that I never need to see the credits to recognize her work, whether in theater release or TV films.

After our fist meeting, I once again failed to follow through with my own writing. I wasn't ready. Not for another thirty years.

Not until now.

9

ON MY OWN

By the late sixties, my relationship with my husband, damaged beyond repair by lack of communication and deceit, as well as the loss of energy that rightfully belonged to my marriage, dissipated by my illicit relationship with Martin, had deteriorated to the point where neither of us could tolerate living together, and we decided to divorce. Our son was by then living on his own, our daughter had just started college away from Los Angeles, so I sold the large home I did not need and could no longer afford, and moved into a tiny apartment. I was living alone for the first time in my life.

About this time, the New Age Movement, with its emphasis on sexual liberation, was bursting out full blown on the California scene, roiling with rebellion against the staid status quo. The nearby Neighborhood Center for Human Development became part of the revolution. It offered such then still unusual seminars and classes as meditation, astrology, aromatherapy, reflexology and phrenology, assertiveness training, and group sexual exploration. Eager to expand my social consciousness horizon, now that I was on my own, I became an active member of the Center.

One of the women I met there invited me to visit a popular, local, family-style, nudist colony, of which she was a member. I swore I would "only look" and was determined to keep on my clothes. But, since everyone else was naked, I felt so conspicuous that I ended up stripping. I lay face down on the towel I had wrapped around myself and surveyed the scene before me.

There were women with single and double mastectomies, hysterectomy and appendectomy scars, painfully thin, as well as grossly obese, men, women, and children of all ages, chatting and walking around, unashamedly unconcerned, letting everything hang out for everyone to see.

A few feet away, I noticed a couple peacefully enjoying the bucolic environment, lying on the lush lawn, she leaning against a tree, reading, while he slept, face up, his head in her lap. Suddenly his flaccid penis became firm, rose up, flopped to one side, then rose up again and flopped to the other side. That was the only sexual activity I saw all day!

I ruefully remembered how I felt when I was obliged to bathe in a tee shirt at Marycliff, warned by the nuns to hide my body even from my own eyes, as though it were something dirty. I exulted in the new feeling of freedom nudity offered, and decided to become a member of the colony.

One of the Neighborhood Center's best lay facilitators, who taught a popular class on "Communication with the Opposite Sex", was a huge and astonishingly ugly black man named Jim McDermott. He was often dressed in all-white jeans and silk shirt, drove a flashy white Cadillac, and was clearly a successful member of the community. He had the softest voice and a gentility about him that earned him everyone's respect, and encouraged us to respond to his message of trust and openness in relationships.

I ended up taking several of Jim's other classes and enjoyed challenging him with many questions. One night, during a class break, Jim asked if I would like to go out with him on a date. My instant inner response was: "He just wants to get into my pants, and if I ever went to bed with him I'd catch the clap!"

I was so horrified at my knee-jerk, racist reaction, that I burst into tears and confessed my prejudice to Jim. He put his huge arms around me, and thanked me for my honesty.

After class, I invited him to my apartment, where we spent hours talking until morning, sharing the significant events of our lives with each other. One of many children, who either died violently or lived desperate lives of poverty and deprivation, he was the only one to escape a similar fate. He graduated from college, owned his own successful real estate firm but was devastated and guilt-ridden that he was unable to help any of his siblings follow his example.

Tragically, Jim, so loving and idealistic, so eager to help transform society, later became involved with Jim Jones' Peoples' Temple cult, and eventually died during their mass-suicide in Guyana in 1979.

During this period of almost compulsive assault on many long-standing sexual taboos, a journalist friend of mine invited me to accompany her, along with several others, on an interview assignment to Sagebrush Point, a notorious sex club on a mountain top that once had been a millionaire's hunting lodge. Although I had heard lurid rumors about Sagebrush Point, I did not really know what to expect, and as long as there was to be a group of us going, I decided to tag along. The scene I walked in on was like something out of *Fellini's Satyricon.* Naked men and women were fondling each other quite explicitly in full view of every-one.

Euphemistically referred-to "Private Sex" was accommodated in the "Ball Room," located on a lower floor. Outfitted with wall-to-wall mattresses, the moans and groans emanating from the nearly total darkness proved that couples were able to focus on fully pleasuring one another, despite the close proximity of others. Another room was used for group sex, where non-participants were invited to observe the activities from the sidelines.

Just as I thought, "Thank God no one I know will see me here," I recognized a psychologist friend and his wife emerging from what looked like a hot, sweaty session below, in the Ball Room! Later, I ran into Sammy Davis Jr. and his wife, stripped down to their multiple gold chains! I could not wait for my friend's interviews to end so we could escape.

Despite this external change in life style and apparent psychological freedom, my own personal situation changed very little. I felt I was living a completely schizophrenic life, still unable to escape Martin's hold on me, despite my efforts to push him away, by taunting him with detailed stories of my adventures. Since I now had an apartment all to myself, there no longer was any need for Martin to have our extra-curricular sessions in his office. He would simply call and invite himself over, whenever he could fit me in, either on his way to the office, or on his way home.

Although I remained sexually inactive outside our relationship, Martin sus-pected the worst, and often angrily insisted I change the bed sheets, certain I had had sex on them with other men! One day, during one of our regular therapy ses-sions in his office, he offered to instruct me in a new method of therapy. He pro-ceeded to explain the process.

"That does not sound new to me," I said. "Haven't we been doing this for a long time?"

"Yes, of course, you and I, we've been testing out my system," he admitted. "I used you because I thought you would make an excellent therapist," he added. "If I train you in this new method, who knows, some day you may want to go back to school and get your own license to practice."

He assured me that he would not be charging me extra for this "training." Of course, I was to continue paying my regular fee for therapy. Martin now began to include minutely explicit letters in our therapy sessions, describing his own sexual fantasies about me, which he often read to me over the phone, between sessions, or at my apartment. As the intensity of our sexual encounters increased, so did my discomfort with the whole process. But soon it all rose to a new level: poems he dedicated to me now began to contain frequent religious references.

This is but one of a series of nine called *"Psalms To My Beloved"*:

No one has loved you more than I.
I assert it.
Neither mother or father,
Brother or sister.
Husband or wife.
And certainly not God Himself.
For I was there when they were not.
Who loved you into the Borderland?
When life was nothing and death a relief.
Was God there? No.
But I was.

Who was there to see your jewels?
To see the torments of your soul?
Its grandeur. Its diving into the abyss?
Was God there? No.
But I was there.
I assert it.
Am I proud? Yes.
For my love, my need.
For my devotion. For my agony.
For love can be, even when God departs.
When God dies, love lives.

So, God be jealous.
For all your power
And your creative grandeur
Look to me. For I love
When You do not!

Under the spell of these heady developments, I was unable to fully focus on the fact that we had not dealt with any of my increasingly more troubling everyday life-problems, not just depression, but my feelings of inadequacy as a mother, having often neglected my children when they needed me most, and my worry about the long-term effect on them after finding me half-dead during the Watts riots.

Despite my exposure to so many new experiences, paradoxically my relationship with Martin became even more all-consuming. The more freedom I had, the more I felt dominated, under his control. The increasingly frequent ups and downs, created by its intensity, remained the primary focus around which everything else faded to insignificance. Nothing else mattered. Eventually, not even the writing. I knew I had to get away before I lost myself completely.

One day Martin announced a friend of his had offered him a mountain cabin to use on his mid-week day off.

"Finally we will actually be able to spend time together," he added, "all alone and away from everything and everybody."

For a while, I was distracted by the excitement over this new dimension to our relationship, and things seemed to become more bearable. All rational warnings were blocked out by the contemplation of actually having the man who dominated both my conscious and unconscious selves all to myself, away from everything painfully familiar, for just a few hours a week. Our once-a-week days together now became the highlight of my life. For months, we had access to a charmingly furnished rustic cabin overlooking a lake, for about twelve hours. Once again my occasional psychic clarity and resolve to break away withered.

Every Thursday, early in the morning, Martin would pick me up at my apartment in his dark green, vintage Jag, and off we would fly towards the mountains, stopping on the way to pick up wine, delicacies like salami, smoked cod, rye bread, cheeses, and fresh squeezed orange juice. Once there, we would pull two cozy sofas from the living room out onto the pine tree-shaded, secluded terrace, jutting out over the lake. By tying the sofa legs together, we created something akin to a cushioned play-pen, and spent hours having sex, eating, drinking and sleeping until evening, when it was time to return to reality and our individual private lives.

This should have been irresistible, the answer to my wildest dreams: the man who had assumed such a critical role in my life had arranged to make me an even more special, concrete part of his. But instead, everything soon became even more painful. After all, nothing had really changed. Everything still remained artificial, risky, secret, and a lie. The closer we were, the more unbearable it felt. But I could not sustain any effort to find a way out from my emotional prison. Fear and addiction always won out.

One afternoon we had fallen asleep on our cabin terrace, and I awoke laughing. My laughter startled my sleeping lover.

"What's so funny?" he asked.

I could not stop laughing. "I had this hilarious dream. We were sleeping here, when I suddenly realized I had wings and started to fly high up! Round and round I flew, with great joy, and called down to you to look up and see me. You looked up at me and said: 'What are you talking about? You're not flying!' 'Yes I am," I insisted. 'No, you're crazy! You're not flying!' you kept saying. I was laughing so hard I woke myself up. Wasn't that a funny dream?"

Martin looked at me with fire in his eyes. "You just made that up!" he screamed, and slapped me hard across my face. No wonder he was so furious. We both knew the dream foreshadowed my ability to finally free myself, promised that someday I would be able to soar away. The slap was so hard it tore my eardrum. For days I walked around, dizzy with vertigo, without a clue as to what was causing my loss of balance. Only when I blew my nose, and felt air coming out of my ear, did I realize what had happened. Martin took me to an ear, nose and throat specialist, far from where either of us lived, and paid for the procedure to repair my eardrum.

Once again, although I had experienced yet another glimmer of hope, a small surge of strength, I could not sustain it for long. Nothing was quite the same after that episode, but I still felt unable to take full control over my life, and our relationship continued.

Although I was still free-lancing as a jewelry designer, by now I had returned to graduate school, hoping that this would occupy my mind enough to allow me to function, but spiritually and psychologically I felt worse than ever. When I once more brought up the subject of quitting therapy, Martin accused me of being ungrateful for all he had done for me.

"Do you realize I have put my life on the line for you, my career, my reputation? And now you want to make all my sacrifices be a waste, count for nothing?"

Each time I attempted to stay away, I was bombarded by letters and poems. Once I even had a one night sexual encounter with a relative stranger, just to see if I could do something unforgivable, and told Martin about it. I also told him what really happened with Abdellatif in Spain, and my near-death during the Watts riots, including my dream. He went into a rage, called me a whore, and accused me of sabotaging our work. When I announced I would not be returning to therapy and would not be going with him to our mountain hideaway the following week, he turned very quiet.

"Don't do this, please. I'm afraid for you! You are still too fragile. You know you can't make it out there without me."

Next day he sent me the following poem:

MY DAY

I miss you,
God, how I miss you!
You are gone
On my day. My day!
Mine? Do I own it?
No, but you gave it.
And took it away.
Blessed be the name of the Lord.
You love today.
Another. My enemy.
As I write, you sleep in his arms.
Stranger? Watts man of unknown identity?
Or love rival?
Man like me, maybe.
Wed.
No matter. I hurt.
I miss you.

I went back again. Still too emotionally dependent, unable to act, I was forced to face the fact that, before I could escape for good, I had to become still stronger. Only much later, after I had gained some distance, did I begin to understand that, not unlike so many victims of family incest, who remain conflicted for years about love and loyalty issues toward their perpetrator, who suffer from confusion about their own role in allowing what occurred to happen, before they are able to attain some measure of clarity and realize IT WAS NOT THEIR FAULT, I was not yet strong enough to confront or escape Martin's control.

◆   ◆   ◆

Meanwhile, I loved attending my graduate school classes and was surprised that my fears about competing with much younger students were unwarranted. While specializing in Art Therapy, I was amazed at the power of this modality to provide quick access to the spontaneous, emotional, non-linear, creative, right side of the brain. By contrast, just talking about a problem often came from its logical, ordered, linear, left side, excluding many of the issues needed for insight and healing.

During my training I produced many drawings that related directly to my psychic status quo. Two of my most powerful drawings were connected, although they occurred about a year apart. The instructor asked the class to show how and where we saw ourselves at that particular time. The first drawing, springing spontaneously from my unconscious, without any pre-conceived intent, shows a woman emerging from the ocean, walking on the beach towards a massive wall surrounding a city. Above the wall she sees a steeple with a cross, a minaret with a crescent, and a dome with a Star of David. In examining the drawing, I recognized that it showed me, emerging from the unconscious (water), only to find a wall prevented me from entering the city that I identified as Jerusalem.

The second drawing, again produced spontaneously, but a year later, depicts the same setting, with one important difference: this time, the wall has a wide crack in it, allowing me possible access to Jerusalem. In my first drawing I showed that I did not yet feel fully entitled to my Jewish identity. The second drawing showed I felt there was hope that some day I would. But not yet: I was still outside the wall.

The most startling part about those two class exercises, was the fact that their unconscious messages were replicated identically, concretely, more than twenty years later, when I actually visited Jerusalem while doing research for *The Mezuzah*. The first time, walking the narrow cobbled streets in the Old City, alone, I felt like a stranger, overwhelmed, disoriented, and convinced I did not belong there. I had prepared two pieces of paper inscribed with wishes to slip into a crack of the Western Wall. I added a third one and wrote: "The next time I visit Jerusalem I want to feel like I belong." When I returned a year later, the feeling of disconnection, of being a stranger, was gone. I felt like a Jew, at home in Jerusalem.

10

FREEDOM at LAST

After I completed my class studies, it was time to choose a site for my clinical internship. I decided to work with terminal patients and their families at a hospice. My task was to counsel, but mostly just listen to them. Parkland was a small hospice unit attached to a suburban medical center. Back in the early seventies, long before most hospice beds went to men dying from AIDS, people were succumbing to common diseases that had been around for centuries, primarily cancer and others, like diabetes or liver and heart failure. End-of-life issues were still considered taboo and were strictly ignored.

My experiences at the hospice proved to be unforgettable. Few of my friends, who often found me in tears after one of my training days, could understand why I would voluntarily subject myself to watching people die. I, myself, did not quite know what drew me to work with patients who knew they had less than six months to live. Maybe, because I had never been close to anyone who had died except *Oma* Jenny, and had, myself, escaped being murdered during the Holocaust, death seemed to be the ultimate mystery. I wanted to know what dying was all about. One day, much later, I suddenly realized that Parkland was the hospital to which I was taken in 1965, near death, after I cut my wrists during the Watts Riots.

Joyce was one of the hospice patients assigned to me. Younger than most of the others, she had an other-worldly beauty: a round, moon-like face, its luminous skin stretched to parchment transparency by all the steroids she had been fed, and huge expressive eyes, set deep in her silk-turbaned, bald head. One would never guess her belly was full of cancer.

"You have six months, at best," the doctor had told Joyce when he urged her to consider checking into a hospice.

Now, four months later, she spent most of her time sleeping or listening to music with her eyes closed. But when I came by, she let me prop her up on pillows, and we would spend hours, drawing pictures showing her cancer devouring her body, others showing the cancer being torn apart by white blood warriors, and talking softly about her nightmares, fears and unfinished business, all the things Joyce could not share with her four young daughters, who went to live with their father and his new wife, after she moved into Parkland.

When I found out Joyce was about to have a birthday, I asked what she'd like me to get for her. "I wish I had pretty nails like yours," she said. "Mine look so awful. I'd love a manicure just once…before…."

"I always do my own, I can do yours," I offered. "That'll be my gift. I'll stop in after your party, Wednesday." Wednesday was not one of Joyce's better days. She needed more medication than usual, and felt particularly weak. The party was hard on her.

"Here comes mama's special cocktail," the nurse announced, just as the children finished helping Joyce open the last of her gifts. "Time to say bye-bye. You know what happens if we wait too long."

Any delay would cause Joyce's pain to become unmanageable, and she was overdue for another dose of morphine. Her girls had tried hard to make it a fun party. They brought gold and silver balloons, red roses from Joyce's favorite bush, cards with poems they had written and clay animals they made in school. But Joyce quickly ran out of energy. Much as she loved them, the children wore her out, and by now she was relieved to see them go. "See you tomorrow," she whispered as she hugged them good-bye. Then she gulped down the pink liquid.

A few minutes later, I arrived with my tray of nail paraphernalia. "Ready for your manicure?" Joyce managed a wan smile. She patted the bed to indicate where she wanted me to set the tray, and reached up for a hug. "Isn't this a hell of a way to spend a birthday?" she cried, spilling tears into my hair. "Just thirty five years! I'm not ready to die!"

This is not like Joyce, I thought. Her initial disbelief and rage at discovering her uterine cancer had escaped detection until it was too late, had turned into quiet resignation by the time we met. After a brief, brave battle through months of chemotherapy, she seemed to have made peace with her fate. Now, that time was running out, her composure was breaking down. I let her cry. I held her for a long time and then sat down next to her. I knew she had done her best to prepare the girls for her death, but the brutal reality of it did not fully hit her until now. "I want to see them grow up," Joyce sobbed as she fell back on her pillow, "I want to be there for their graduations, their weddings, their babies, I want to be a grandmother!"

I felt helpless. In my brief time at Parkland, I quickly discovered that a hospice is not a place where miracles are likely to happen: no one gets out alive. How do you comfort someone who is dying so long before her time, I wondered? Could anything I might say possibly make any difference? While groping for words, I began preparing Joyce's left hand for their first coat of pink enamel.

"Joyce," I whispered after a long silence. "You're right. This is a rotten deal. It is so unfair! You deserve to live a full lifetime. But perhaps it is not how long you live that really matters, but how many important, meaningful things happened to you during your life. What's the most wonderful experience you can remember?"

Joyce closed her eyes. She strained to concentrate. Then her face suddenly came aglow with a dazzling smile. Eyes still closed, she murmured, "Giving birth...bringing my babies to life...feeling them push their way out...God! It was so beautiful! I can still feel the miracle of it!" As the morphine cocktail began to take effect, I watched Joyce slip into a deep drug-induced daze, while I continued applying the finishing touches to her nails.

Next day I arrived on the ward earlier than usual. One of the nurses intercepted me. "Hurry, Joyce has been asking for you."

I rushed to Joyce's bedside. She seemed to be asleep, but when I touched her hand, she opened her eyes. They looked glazed and delirious, as she strained to focus. Now she recognized me and smiled.

"Guess what?" she whispered, excitement in her voice as she reached up to pull me close. "The pains, they're just two minutes apart!...Fast, like before, with the others.... Some of us are just meant to have babies!...Ah, here comes another one!"

Saying this, she grabbed my hand, placed it on her distended belly, arched back into her pillow, and let out a soft groan. I could feel her bearing down, pushing, pushing hard. "Here it comes now!"

A deep, deep breath, one long, low moan, and I suddenly felt Joyce's body relax. I looked down at her face, still smiling, but strangely serene now. The strain was gone. I remained there, my hand on Joyce's belly, for a long time. I did not take her pulse as I was supposed to. I did not have to. I knew Joyce was gone.

◆   ◆   ◆

By now I was close to completing all the requirements for my Master's Degree. Although I was still "in therapy" with Martin, slowly, bit by bit, I learned to assert myself more, to talk back, to argue, to challenge what used to be law. I returned to my writing. My inner bird was flapping its wings, getting ready to fly.

Oddly enough, when the final break happened, it was Martin who took the initiative. On Valentine's Day, 1975, I received a letter from him, telling me he could no longer stand the pain we were inflicting on each other and pleaded with me to just let go! He ended the letter with: "Please do not destroy." Although finally free, it took a long time, working with several other therapists, to repair the psychic damage caused by my relationship with Martin. Each of them urged me to place a formal complaint with the Bureau of Behavioral Sciences. All expressed outrage at the breach of his sacred trust and his arrogance in controlling and using me for his own gratification, while charging me for his services. Despite what I went through, I nevertheless had a hard time fully accepting the fact that I was a victim of gross therapist abuse, and it took other professionals a long time to convince me that, despite the fact that I admitted collaborating, succumbing to the seduction, and enjoying much of it, an ethical therapist should never have encouraged or allowed what happened.

One of the therapists I worked with, in a letter he hoped I would use in my formal accusation of abuse, referred to my fourteen years under Martin's control, as "another Holocaust." But all I wanted now was to move ahead, look at my new options, and get as far away from any bad memories as possible. The last thing I wanted was to devote any more time than absolutely necessary to the painful past. It took another seventeen years before I was ready to personally confront Martin. By then I had a new life.

11

MIRACLE in TAOS, NEW MEXICO

In July 1975, a few months after all contact with Martin had ceased, I received an invitation to attend the opening in Taos of an art show honoring an old friend, Jim Meek. Jim had saved my sanity more than twenty years earlier, when he and my family were stationed at Camp Gordon, an army post, hospital, and prison in Augusta, Georgia, during the Korean War. Although my husband was an officer, and Jim an enlisted man, and fraternization was strictly forbidden, we discretely "adopted" Jim, because the three of us seemed to have a lot in common, rare among army personnel on that godforsaken outpost, such as an interest in literature, psychology, and the arts.

We began by occasionally inviting Jim to dinner, and quickly learned that our friend was not only a highly knowledgeable student of history, but also a talented musician and artist. During our three years in Augusta, we grew close, and remained so long after all of us left army life behind. Back in the early fifties, Augusta was a veritable cultural wasteland, a bastion of social exclusiveness, restrictions, and racism. Among several personal experiences were the frightening reactions from white bystanders when I once innocently drank from a "Colored" drinking fountain, and again upon entering a "Colored Only" waiting room at the train station, shortly after arriving in the South.

Our next-door neighbors, in a residential area close to the base, were a couple with two small children. The husband was a professor on sabbatical from Duke University, and his wife was a full-time homemaker. My hope for a neighborly relationship was quickly dashed, when they stopped allowing their children to associate with ours, because they had observed that the black cleaning lady, whom I had picked up in town, was allowed to sit next to me in my car, and enter the front door of my home. "We don't do that here!" they warned me, forbade their children to play with ours, and avoided all contact with us after that.

Jim, although he, himself, was a southerner from Kentucky, sympathized with our liberal beliefs and understood well the resulting lack of social acceptance. He encouraged me to channel my frustration into creativity, and offered to teach me to paint. We spent many a night working through to early morning, deeply absorbed in some fascinating art project. His enthusiastic support and companionship made my otherwise almost unbearable time in Augusta an experience I now look back on with pleasure.

Upon his release from the service, Jim moved to Taos, and eventually opened his own art gallery. He soon became successful, representing a number of well-known fellow-artists. Although I was long divorced by the time he invited me to attend his own art opening in early September of 1975, we had maintained our relationship with many letters and occasional visits.

When I arrived in Taos, I found Jim's red adobe hacienda aglow with cut aluminum and stained glass lanterns hanging from wooden beams, wrought iron candelabra lit with fragrant candles tucked into hollowed-out niches in deep orange walls, cushy *Kilim*-style tapestry-upholstered sofas and chairs, Pueblo rugs on floors and hung on walls, and all kinds of local folk art—such the shiny, black, etched pottery created by María, a famed Indian potter, intricately woven baskets, and a museum-quality collection of *Kachina* dolls.

Everywhere I looked, I found a feast for the eyes, featuring not only Jim's own paintings but also those of other local artists. In addition to me, Jim had invited other close artist friends, including several out-of-towners who used to live in Taos, to spend the night as his guests before the art opening next day.

Jim proved to be a delightful host and excellent cook. He served a mouth-watering southwestern buffet supper of homemade *chile rellenos* filled with spicy melted cheese and chives, fresh *cilantro*-garnished *guacamole, pollo mole,* tender chicken soaking in its mysterious chocolate sauce, *tamales* filled with marinated shredded beef, wrapped in blackened corn husks, steamed rice with chopped red *chiles* and tiny green peas, and *sopaipillas,* those irresistible deep-fried, puffy, chewy rolls, waiting to be slathered in butter and dipped in honey. For dessert he offered *flan* swimming in burned sugar, with plenty of fruity *sangria,* beer and *vino tinto* to wash it all down.

The dinner conversation sparkled with wit and nostalgia, revolving primarily around Taos history, shared memories, and personal experiences. One story emerged, again and again, in various versions: the influence, moral and even financial support offered to most struggling local artists by a female fellow-painter they simply referred to as "our angel." Jim brought out several old photographs, showing her, surrounded by some of the artists present at the table: a tiny, striking-looking lady, wearing fringed shawls over peasant blouses and long skirts, her head always swathed in a turban with a jewel pinned above her forehead.

I excused myself long before the others stopped partying, eager to get up bright and early next morning to help Jim hang his show and prepare the gallery for the opening. But Jim told me he had plenty of help, and urged me to use the time to explore Taos.

"Here's a map of the city," he said, and told me to return by about five in the afternoon.

I welcomed the opportunity to wander around town, and took my time to walk to the city center, the Taos Plaza, renowned for its underground police station. Circled by street vendors displaying silver jewelry laid out on colorful *serapes*, gift shops and restaurants catering to ever-present tourists, I found myself facing the entrance of a charming old hotel called *La Fonda de Taos*.

What caught my attention immediately was a poster propped up on an easel outside the hotel lobby advertising: "INSIDE: AUTHENTIC, BANNED EROTIC PAINTINGS BY FAMOUS AUTHOR AND PAINTER D. H. LAWRENCE. ENTRANCE FEE $2.00."

Now, I am no authority on D. H. Lawrence, although I had read many of his novels and was familiar with various well-known facts about his life and tempestuous marriage to Frieda, during the years they lived in Taos. I also knew he had created some rather provocative paintings. One fact I felt certain of was that, in 1929, during an uproar generated by his most famous novel, *Lady Chatterly's Lover*, all Lawrence's sexually explicit paintings were judged obscene in England and burned. Feeling outraged at what was clearly a lie aimed at defrauding unsuspecting tourists, I charged into the lobby and asked to speak to the manager. An official-looking young woman soon appeared and introduced herself.

"Maybe some of the tourists you manage to lure into your establishment are gullible enough to believe your claims," I said in my most supercilious, superior-sounding tone, "but I happen to know these forgeries could not possibly be painted by D. H. Lawrence because the real ones were all burned years ago."

The hotel manager accepted my challenge to her integrity with unsettling calm.

"Despite what you and many others assume, a few of the paintings managed to escape the fire. Museum authorities have authenticated them. We have them on display upstairs. Would you like to see them?"

My unresolved skepticism only slightly displaced by curiosity, I accepted her invitation, paid my two dollars, and climbed the stairs to the second floor. The room displaying the paintings was rather small for a gallery, and not at all well lit. At one end, sitting behind a desk, was a man absorbed in a book, whom I took to be a guard. He did not bother to acknowledge my presence as I entered.

I was touched by the paintings' sweetly sensual nature, not at all lurid or offensive by today's, and even 1970s', standards. What startled me, was the number of photographs attached to the wall between the paintings, each showing a group of, what I assumed, were Taos locals, each showing in their midst the very woman Jim and his friends had described and praised during last night's dinner: tiny, wearing long, ethnic garb, and always with her hair covered by a jeweled turban. I did not remember anyone mentioning her name, since they kept referring to her only as "our angel," so I approached the guard. He remained absorbed by his book.

"I am here to attend Jim Meek's art opening at Gallery A tonight. Last night all Jim's friends were talking about this wonderful woman. Who is she?"

He looked up.

"Her name is Noula Karavas. Many of her paintings are displayed throughout the hotel."

"Oh, yes, I remember now they mentioned she was a painter, too. And what is her connection to Lawrence's paintings?"

"She lived here when the Lawrences did. By the way," he added, "I am Saki Karavas. Noula is my mother."

My interest was instantly aroused. "You are Greek," I said.

I remembered Nico telling me, long ago, that he had spent some time in Taos, shortly after his baby son died, hoping to fight his depression in a place far away from anything familiar. He might even have stayed at the same hotel, I mused, since Greeks always seem to find one another anywhere in the world. It had been years since I had last heard from Nico, and, for a moment, a wave of sadness and longing swept over me.

What struck me most about Saki were his piercing black eyes. He was also totally bald and, when he emerged from behind the desk to kiss my hand, I saw that, although he was not tall, he was quite handsome and elegant in his gray silk pants, matching shirt, and paisley ascot. I guessed him to probably be in his early fifties.

"How did you happen to get permission to display these paintings?" I asked.

"I own this hotel," he said. "I also own the paintings."

"Really?" He was so matter of fact and casual, I had no doubt he was telling me the truth. "Why and how did you acquire the paintings?"

"I have been a great admirer of Lawrence for a long time," he explained. "My mother also met Frieda and some of the other women who were connected to him: Mabel Dodge Luhan, Lady Dorothy Brett, and Millicent Rogers, who all lived here in Taos when the Lawrences did. When the paintings were judged obscene and threatened with destruction, some of them were smuggled out of England. When they became available, I bought them."

"And your mother," I asked. "She must have been a remarkable woman. When did she pass away?"

"She is old but still very much alive. She lives upstairs, here, in the hotel."

When he saw the delight in my eyes, he added:

"Would you like to meet her?"

Saki took my hand and led me up another flight of stairs, and knocked on one of the doors.

"*Mana mou,* it's Saki with a guest who would like to meet you. May we enter?"

An almost inaudible voice said something I did not understand.

"Mama and I usually converse in Greek. But, don't worry, she speaks perfect English. She loves to receive company. Here, let me introduce you."

When Saki opened the door, my eyes first had to get used to the near-darkness in the room. Against one wall, there was a tiny bed, covered in red velvet, matching the flocked, red velvet on the walls. Red brocade drapes nearly shut out the light. Several wrought-iron and stained glass lanterns hung low from strategically placed ceiling chains, and carved and inlaid wooden chests, glass bowls, vases and other folk art objects were scattered haphazardly all about the room. A tiny woman, wrapped in an embroidered shawl, sat in a rocking chair in one corner, next to one of the windows, her feet resting on a red silk pillow.

"*Mana mou,* this lady heard about you last night. She would like to hear some of your stories."

Noula held out her hand and motioned me to sit on a low stool next to her.

"Come child, come close so we can talk."

Everything about Noula was striking. Her face was heavily lined but her eyes were animated like those of a young woman: clear and the color of dark brown amber with flecks of gold. The turban covering most of her hair was of turquoise silk chiffon, and the brooch pinned to it, above her forehead, was a cluster of coral cabochons. Yellow, Turkish, embroidered silk slippers covered her tiny feet.

Saki now kissed his mother's forehead and turned to me: "You and Mama have a nice chat," he said, walking towards the door. "I have a meeting to go to, and I will pick you up later and we'll have lunch together." He paused, then added: "I too have been invited to Jim's show and plan to be there tonight."

Before I could say anything, he was gone. Without asking my name or any information about me, Noula now began to pour out a litany of stories that left me increasingly puzzled: each detailed incidents that happened in Taos that she herself had witnessed, tales of heroism, good deeds, generosity, kindness to strangers, and even unexplained miracles.

Although I cannot recall all the pertinent details, I do remember that, what the stories all had in common, was that the protagonist in each was a Jew—a doctor, who brought a critically ill child to a specialist in another town and thus saved his life; a teacher, who adopted a mentally ill and abused student; a grocer, who regularly and anonymously brought food to the impoverished Pueblo Indians, so as not to hurt their pride; an artist, who cared for a housebound elderly couple, offering services such as house-keeping and shopping; and the town whore who lovingly, sexually initiated two teenage brothers, sons of a regular client, who were too shy to approach a girl.

Some events went back sixty or more years! As she spoke, I watched Noula becoming more and more agitated, as though possessed by some kind of demon who was forcing her to spill out her stories. Then, as suddenly as she began, she stopped, closed her eyes, and leaned back in total exhaustion. I was puzzled by what I had just witnessed, concerned about the old lady and at a loss what to do or say. What is this all about? I wondered. Why all these stories about Jewish heroes? Did she know I was a Jew? How could she? Not even Saki knew my name. None of it made any sense. Finally I blurted out the first thing that came to mind:

"I am Jewish, but the great love of my life was Greek. He broke my heart. I have not seen him in almost thirty years."

Noula suddenly burst into tears.

"Come, let me hold you," she whispered, and wrapped her arms around me as I knelt next to her. "I did not understand why I felt this compulsion to tell you these stories, why I had to remember every Jew whose life had touched mine…But now I realize why: I had to heal something Greek in you."

I did not understand what she meant, but I felt deeply moved by her emotion and I just allowed myself to let her warmth envelop me. When Saki returned, he found us quietly sitting with our arms around each other.

"*Mana mou*, are you alright? Perhaps you need to take a nap. I brought you some *musaka* and *dolmades*, if you are hungry. My friend and I are going out to lunch now."

Saki kissed Noula on the forehead. She took both my hands in hers, held them very lightly, and looked deep into my eyes.

"You will tell me about it, please?"

I wanted to ask, 'tell you about what?' but I somehow trusted that I would discover what she meant when "it" happened.

"Yes, of course I will."

"Your mother…she…she…," I stammered when Saki closed the door.

"I see she made a connection with you. I am glad. We both know nothing happens by chance. And yes, she has a gift. Some people call her a psychic, but I just believe she has such a loving heart that she is able to reach into the deepest corner of another's soul. It does not happen with everybody, only some people with whom she has a spiritual bond. She must have felt one with you."

"But she knows nothing about me."

"Her knowing comes from a deeper source. It is a gift."

I found myself being very quiet during lunch. Much to my embarrassment, I could barely keep my eyes open. My experience with Noula had left me drained. Saki was sensitive enough to recognize my condition.

"Why don't I take you to my apartment, at the hotel, so you can take a nap. I have things to do, so I will leave you alone and wake you up in time to take you to Jim's place for the opening."

I was too wiped out to do anything but say thank you, grateful for the chance to be alone, to absorb what had just happened. My trust in Saki's word was not misplaced. All I remember about getting to his place is collapsing on a wonderfully comfortable bed and Saki covering me with a silky comforter. He closed the drapes and quietly let himself out.

I awoke to find Saki sitting on the edge of the bed, smiling at me.

"You have slept for three hours," he said. How do you feel now?"

I felt totally disoriented: what was I doing in this stranger's bed? Who was he? Then, slowly, some things began to fall in place.

"Remember me?" he asked, a bemused look on his face. "I'm Saki. You spoke to my mother. It must have really affected you. It always does…would you like something to drink? It might help wake you up."

"What time is it?" I asked.

"Almost time to go to Jim's show. If you like, you can use my shower to freshen up. You got a bit rumpled. I have a closet full of all kinds of traditional, ethnic skirts, tops, and shawls you might want to try."

I must have looked really dazed, and he laughed.

"Don't worry. I am not trying to get you naked, although I'm tempted. I am offering you what I have on hand, for hotel guests to use for festivals."

I accepted Saki's offer. He was a perfect gentleman and gave me total privacy. I picked out a turquoise crinkled skirt with a multi-colored peasant blouse and a pale peach, fringed, silk shawl. Saki loaned me a beautiful turquoise necklace and matching earrings, ("my mother's," he explained). I packed my own clothes into a small bag, and off we went to Jim's opening. As exciting as it was—music, dancing, wonderful food, with Saki hovering over me like a protective angel—nothing came close to my experience with Noula. Being with her had fed my soul, and I was grateful to savor and take it all home with me to treasure forever.

When I was about to leave Taos next day, Saki came to say good-bye.

"I wish we could have spent more time together. It would have been so exciting to make love with you. Here, I brought you a photo, so you won't forget me, and perhaps it will happen the next time we meet," he said.

The picture showed a broadly smiling Saki, a large flower pinned to his tuxedo jacket, a cigar in one hand and a stuffed puppy in the other, no shirt, and only a white towel wrapped around his middle, above shapely, hairy legs. It captured his spirit perfectly. Saki called me several times during the next few years, each time to invite me to meet him in some exotic place like Buenos Aires (he was a fabulous tango dancer) or Calcutta, or Rio de Janeiro, vowing to show me the most exciting time of my life, to make up for our lost opportunity in Taos, but I always declined, though part of me was certainly tempted.

Every once in a while I came across stories about Saki in various travel publications, telling of his notorious bachelor exploits, his many love affairs with movie stars and other famous beauties, which earned him the title of "Don Juan of Taos," all emphasizing his special contributions to the mystique and mystery of Taos. No one even mentioned Noula.

Many years later I happened to be in Taos, to give a lecture on the New Mexico Crypto-Jews, and rushed to find Saki. The hotel looked the same, and when I asked to see Saki, the lobby attendant pointed to a vacant-eyed old man, sitting on a chair in the lobby, waving to guests passing by.

"He has Alzheimer's," she whispered. "His mother died a few years ago. We are his only family".

I walked up to Saki, put my arms around him, and kissed him on the fore-head.

He smiled.

I left and burst into tears.

12

A NEW LIFE

Although I did not understand how or why, what happened to me in Taos had a profound effect on me. I returned home determined to take control of my life. Although it would take more than a year of therapy, with other professionals, to repair the damage to my self-confidence and ability to make positive choices, so crippled during the past fourteen years, everything in me was now mobilized to reverse the status quo. I decided I needed to do something dramatic to symbolize the change I was now committed to set in motion—something outrageous and brave, and unlike anything I had ever done before. My experience with Noula reminded me of how much I missed Nico, whom I had not seen for so long, and although I knew I would never find anyone like him, I decided to look for a new love. I was determined to find an effective way to draw attention to my search.

Although using personal ads, placed in newspapers, had long been a socially acceptable way to meet potential mates throughout Europe, back in the seventies the only publication I knew of in the Los Angeles area that offered anything like it was a throw-away rag called *The Free Press*, whose ads were notorious for their primarily deviant sexual content. I was certainly never going to display my ad in *The Free Press*.

I called the *Los Angeles Times,* and asked for the advertising department manager.

"I would like to place a personal ad," I announced.

"Lady, I think you're calling the wrong paper. WE don't do personal ads."

"I know. Maybe it's time you did. That's how nice people meet each other in Europe."

"Madam, this is the U.S. of America. WE don't do that here."

"Well, this is your opportunity to be a pioneer. It's hard for singles to meet in a large city like Los Angeles. Can you think of a more effective way for people to find one another—anonymously at first, using a postal box and pseudonym, describing the important qualities desired, communicating by phone for a while, sorting out what fits and feels right and what does not, until each decides it is okay to finally meet face to face in some safe public place?"

"Whoever you are, you don't seem to hear me. I told you, this is not Europe, and we don't do personals, and we never will."

I was not about to give up so easily. I now wrote a letter to the *Los Angeles Times*, c/o Publisher, reiterating my position, and asking to meet with him.

A few days later, I found a message on my answering machine, from someone at the *Los Angeles Times*, inviting me to come downtown to their editorial offices the following week.

"Please bring along a letter from your attorney, your physician, and your clergyman, vouching for your health and character."

At first I could not help laughing. What did they think I was, a hooker? Then my heart started to pound. What had I set in motion? Would I be able to hold my own with these possibly hostile, suspicious, sexist bigwigs? My brain began to churn. What in the world would I say in an ad?

I spent the next several days composing my ad. Then I called my daughter-in-law in Arizona, who happened to be an alternative healer and astrologer. Although she had been amazingly accurate and effective once or twice before, I did not quite believe in either discipline, but I felt that I needed whatever help I could get to see me through my adventure. It couldn't hurt, could it?

"I want you to look at my chart" I told her, "and find the most romantically promising date for me, during the next few weeks."

When she called me back, she did not ask any questions but had an answer ready.

"The most propitious day is pretty close, Sunday, October 5. It looks really good on your chart." Sunday. That meant the *Times* would include a magazine, book review, and the excellent *Calendar* section I always made a point to read first. It covered all the arts, classical music, theater, architecture, as well as a great jazz section. I figured, that's where men were most likely to go, and that's where I wanted my ad to appear.

I arrived at the *Times'* building dressed sedately in a navy suit, armed with letters from an attorney friend, a rabbi who had married one of my friends, and my doctor, who vouched for both my mental and physical health. Three men greeted me and introduced themselves: the publisher, the editor in chief, and the advertising editor. The room, where we met, was a small conference room, adjoining the busy, noisy pressroom. When I walked in, all eyes turned towards me, and I felt myself blush and become slightly light-headed. We sat down and I handed over my letters of recommendation. They took turns reading each one, while I sat, trying to find in their faces some clue to their reactions. There was nothing to read. Their expressions were blank.

"Well, now, you are quite a determined young lady," one of them began. "Do you ever take no for an answer?"

"Not if I believe in fighting for what I am trying to achieve."

"And you believe personal ads are worth fighting for, even though no decent publication has dared to tackle that slippery issue?"

"Well, that is not exactly true. As I wrote in my letter, in other parts of the world the use of personal ads is a tested and honorable way to reach out to and connect with others one might otherwise never meet."

"And why did you choose the *Los Angeles Times* for your rather questionable experiment?"

"The *Times* is renowned for its excellent reputation, many awards, and innovative spirit. That makes it the logical choice for pioneering this public service. I am certain it is bound to bring you a huge new readership. Others will soon follow your example, but you will always have the honor of having been the first truly respectable mainstream publication to reach out to Los Angeles' huge singles population."

They looked at each other for what seemed a long time.

"And where and when would you want your ad to appear?"

"Sunday, October 5, in the jazz section of the *Calendar*."

The publisher immediately reacted.

"But we cannot run a personal ad in the *Calendar*! We have never done anything like that before!"

"The *Calendar* section will give both my ad and the *Times* credibility and prestige. What better place to launch your new service!"

They looked each other again. This time I detected one slight nod after another.

"You seem to be well prepared. I assume you have composed your ad."

I nodded and handed over five carefully typed paragraphs, with a bold black border around it:

DO YOU KNOW THIS MAN?

Dynamic. Aware. Articulate. Vigorous. Past his middle forties. Secure, yet open, still growing. Liberal, a humanist, in touch with his feelings. Appreciates leisure but is turned on by his work. Used to a relaxed, gracious lifestyle revolving around good friends, books, art, music, and good conversation over good food, travel, theater, concerts, and film.

Passionate yet gentle, he values honesty, communicates at gut level. Has warmth, intimacy, and a full life to share with that special woman who offers zest for living with a capacity for love.

WHO WOULD PLACE SUCH AN AD?

She happens to be a rather unusual woman who finds the haphazard L.A. dating scene a boring and dehumanizing waste of time, yet likes herself well enough to believe deeply that such a man exists for her.

She is a vibrant, attractive 5'5" divorcee. Artistic. Multilingual. European background. She is unencumbered, an exceptionally youthful 47, with a fulfilling, flexible career. She knows how to live alone, creatively, but misses the joy that comes from sharing the mysteries of living and the magic of loving one person who cares and matters above all others.

If you know this man, or think you might be the one, please send a detailed letter to BOXZ212-DA. Photo appreciated.

They passed the sheet from one to the other, and I waited patiently until each one had read it. They kept looking at me, then down at the ad, and again at each other.

Finally one of them spoke.

"Do you have any idea what such an ad would cost, especially in the *Calendar* section?"

"I don't know, but I am sure it won't be cheap. Maybe a couple of hundred dollars. I am prepared to pay that."

The man laughed.

"It'll most likely be double that. Can you afford to pay that? Up front?"

"So, you are willing to run my ad?" I asked.

"Well…We still have to discuss this further, before making a final decision. You realize, this would be quite revolutionary for our paper. We'll let you know."

As I drove home, I kept telling myself not to count on anything. After all, he date I had selected was just three weeks away. That gave them very little time to arrive at a decision. But two days later, I received an invoice from the *Times,* requesting a certified check for $465.00, spelling out my ad just as I wrote it, and specifying exactly what page in the Jazz section of the *Calendar* it would appear on Sunday, October 5, 1975.

On that special day I awoke before 4 A.M., knowing the newsboy usually delivered the Sunday paper quite early. I tore through the *Calendar* section, and there was my ad, elegantly outlined in black, just as I had planned, at 3' x 2.5' even more impressive than I had dared hope.

Four days later, the mailman delivered a fat manila envelope from the *Los Angeles Times*, the first of several packets I was to receive over the next few days. It contained twenty-three letters, all written on October 5, the same day my ad appeared. Obviously, the writers were eager to respond. I was impressed with the letters' quality and honesty. Most were very complimentary and the writers were of varying backgrounds, mostly professionals. Some actually included photos. Two expressed suspicion, wanting to know if I represented some kind of a company, recruiting men for questionable pursuits. Three were from women, asking for my LEFTOVERS! Separately, not included in the manila envelope from the *Times,* and in no way connected to my ad, were several other pieces of mail, mostly bills and advertisements, which I looked at only after I had read all the responses to my ad..

ONE WAS A LETTER FROM NICO!

It was mailed from Chicago and dated Sunday, October 5, 1975. He explained that his wife had recently died and asked if he could come to California to meet me and my family. Several days earlier, he had contacted my mother, who still lived in the same West End Ave apartment where he and I had fallen in love so long ago. This time Mama told him where to find me. She obviously never mentioned that I was divorced.

That night I wrote to Noula: "'IT' happened! Your magic worked. My Greek love, who broke my heart so long ago, is back in my life! Thank you, and may God bless you!" I re-read Nico's letter over and over again, in utter disbelief. His handwriting was the same as I remembered it from so many years ago. Like those old letters, he signed it "All my love."

13

FACE to FACE

First came heart-pounding excitement. To actually see Nico again, after so many years, was the fulfillment of long-abandoned dreams. When the reality of it hit me, my breath froze in my throat. Is he expecting me to look the way I did, when we fell in love, more than three decades ago? Will we even recognize each other? How will he react when he finds out I am no longer married? It took a while to calm my racing brain enough to think clearly. Although Nico enclosed his telephone number, I decided not to call him, afraid of what I might blurt out, feeling it would be safer to write a letter, tell him I am divorced, and enclose a snapshot, so he will recognize me. Or change his mind.

I wrote him that I was excited to hear from him, looking forward to his visit, and would be glad to pick him up at the airport whenever he decided to make the trip west. I added that I would arrange for him to stay at a nearby hotel, because I lived alone, in a tiny apartment. I hoped that this information would ease some of the tension both of us were sure to feel. The snapshot I enclosed was a rather flattering one of myself, wearing a print chiffon gown, showing an impressively low décolleté.

His response came just a few days later: "Wow! This sure is a whole new ball-game! You are still beautiful, after all these years, and I would have recognized you in a crowd in an instant! Can't wait to see you." A few days later I received his itinerary, with an arrival date set for sometime in mid-November. Six weeks!

"Sorry I can't make it any sooner," he wrote. "It takes time for me to break away. My daughter still lives with me, and Mama depends on me to help out. But I'm making arrangements to have others in my family take care of everything while I am gone. I don't have a recent photo to send, so you'll just have to take a chance on me, sight unseen."

Actually, I ended up welcoming the extra time, to prepare myself for Nico's arrival. I had not quite realized how anxious I was. I felt I needed to calm down.

But we both soon felt brave enough to chat by phone, catching up with each other's lives, and helping one another get more and more comfortable with the prospect of meeting face to face. In the meantime, I answered all the letters I received in response to my ad, explaining, as gently as I could, that I had met a man on whom I wanted to focus my efforts to create a relationship.

Amazingly, just a few weeks later, another person, this time a man, copied my format almost identically, and succeeded in posting his own personal ad in the *Los Angeles Times Calendar* section! Eventually, a twice-weekly singles column called *"Dateline"* appeared in the weekend editions of the *Los Angeles Times* for several years, followed by similar ventures, in hundreds of other reputable mainstream publications, both newspapers and magazines.

I don't know how I got through the day Nico was due to arrive. Excitement and terror alternated in pulling and pushing me from dizzying emotional highs to precipitous lows. It all finally narrowed down to worrying about something as prosaic as what to wear. After trying on several outfits, I decided to keep things "California casual", and settled on blue jeans and a matching jacket over a hot pink silk shell.

I arrived at the airport well before I needed to and, long before the post 9/11 security restrictions made air travel a nightmare, I was allowed to wait just outside the arrival gate. As soon as the incoming passengers began rushing into the waiting area, I stepped way back and found a pillar to lean against for support. And suddenly, there he was. Bigger than I remembered, his black hair salt and pepper now, but just as full, his face ruggedly craggy. He stood still, looked around, and when his eyes found me, he flashed that heart-stopping, toothy grin. He dropped his suitcase and slowly ambled towards me. I met him halfway, and when we were face to face, he enveloped me in his arms. I felt faint, breathing in his musky smell, still intoxicatingly familiar after so many years.

"It's really you," I whispered.

I don't know how long we remained there, like that, wrapped up in each other, but when we finally let go, a ring of people stood there, smiling at us. It brought back an old memory of a time when Nico came to spend a weekend with my family the summer they had rented a cottage for two weeks at Lake Mahopac. One afternoon Nico and I took a long walk along the lake. As an elderly couple passed us, I heard the woman whisper to her husband: "Das ist ein goldiges Paerchen."

I giggled and translated: "They said in German "What an adorable couple!" Nico smiled and enfolded me in his arms the same way he just did at the airport, three decades later.

I drove Nico to his hotel, and then brought him to my apartment for a broiled lobster dinner. We ended up curled up on my sofa, sipping wine, and talking, non-stop, for hours. Although he held my hand and occasionally caressed my face, I was surprised and disappointed that he seemed rather shy and reluctant to go beyond that. He ended up falling asleep, his head on my shoulder. I managed to get up without waking him, slipped a pillow under his head, covered him with a quilt, and spent the night alone in my bedroom.

I got up several times during the night, just to look at Nico, to make sure I wasn't dreaming, but there he was, softly snoring, wrapped up in my blanket in the living room. "Damn it, what a waste," I thought, mentally stomping my foot, barely resisting the urge to crawl under the covers with him. "After all this time, there is no valid reason to stop us from finally making love. I've waited long enough!"

Nico looked a bit sheepish, next morning, when my puttering around in the kitchen woke him up.

"Sorry…I didn't mean to…I guess I was just too tired last night."

He saw the puzzled look on my face.

"The truth is, I really wanted to make love to you, but I find am not quite ready for that. My wife only died six months ago, and I did not realize I still feel married. I would feel like I'm cheating…Can you understand that?"

My tender feelings for this sweet, old-fashioned man, swept away my disappointment. Was this innate decency not part of what I fell in love with so many years ago?

I put my arms around Nico. "I wasn't going to tell you, but I nearly raped you last night," I whispered, "but guess I'll have to put that off for a while."

We both laughed.

After breakfast Nico asked how I would feel about taking a few days off, to get away from the city.

"In Chicago it is already winter. Here it is still warm. Would it not be wonderful to spend some time somewhere on the coast, walk along the beach, like the first time we met in Asbury Park?"

That afternoon we drove to Laguna Beach, a charming, small art colony, and, by dusk, we decided to check into the Sea Lodge Inn, because all its upstairs rooms faced the ocean. My heart sank when Nico rented TWO SEPARATE ROOMS!!! I tried my best not to show my disappointment. Our adjoining rooms did not even have a connecting inside door, but they did share a narrow veranda that ran along the full length of the Lodge, past every room overlooking the beach below.

We spent the next three days being lazy, walking, sharing more and more intimate details of our lives, picnicking in the sand, dancing in little clubs, growing slowly bolder in expressing our physical hunger. But every night, after holding each other in a passionate embrace at my door, Nico said good night and retreated to his room! I alternated between mentally clawing at the wall separating our rooms and crying myself to sleep in frustration.

The fourth night, a knock on the glass veranda door startled me awake. I pulled open the blinds. There stood Nico, tousled-haired, sleepy-eyed, wrapped in a short black and white Japanese *hapi* coat. I held my breath as I pulled back the sliding door. Nico hesitated a moment before walking in.

"This is ridiculous!" he whispered as he picked me up and carried me to my bed. All our pent-up sexual energy now burst out like a sudden summer storm, with lightning and thunder and a violent tornado crescendo followed by a steamy, sweaty calm. I don't know how long we lay there, fully spent, but we finally fell asleep in each other's arms.

There was nothing shy or tentative about the way Nico had finally taken possession of me. Deliciously raunchy, fully focused on pleasuring me, knowing instinctively where and how to touch me while bringing us both to total release, it all felt so completely natural, so effortlessly balanced, one would have assumed that years of shared practice had preceded it.

When Nico awoke, it was early morning.

"Let's take a walk," he whispered, kissing me awake as I stirred in his embrace. "It's too beautiful outside to stay indoors."

The Lodge's ground floor terrace, facing the beach, was surrounded by a three-foot high stucco retaining wall to keep out the sand. Nico went ahead, and, as I began to climb over the wall, he lifted me up, swung me over, and whispered: "Now I don't have to envy the fence anymore!"

Everything felt so easy and natural, I was puzzled and unprepared when Nico announced he had to return to Chicago the next day, sooner than he had originally planned. Saying good-bye was very hard, but even harder was the fact that I did not hear from Nico, and was unable to reach him for nearly a week. What had gone wrong? Had our passionate lovemaking spooked him, was he still feeling disloyal to this dead wife after all?

When he finally called, he explained the reason for his early departure: the sudden excitement of being with me had set off the manic phase of his bipolar condition, and he ended up in the hospital for several days after his return.

"Although I am on lithium and am being carefully monitored, I have learned to lead a rather calm life, if I don't want to end up unable to sleep for days on end and acting grandiose. I am not used to what happened to me with you, getting all stirred up. And I am still filled with guilt that my wife had to deal with my craziness for years, before I was on medication. I keep wondering if that might have precipitated her cancer."

Despite these potential pitfalls, we were both determined to see one another as often as our private lives and obligations allowed, while taking into consideration Nico's medical condition. In the meantime, we kept the phone lines buzzing.

The next time Nico came west, it was the following February, for my Master's degree graduation. The party that followed, at my home, gave all my friends the opportunity to meet the man I had loved for so many years. Everyone was happy for me, and complimented me on my good fortune, praising his personality, sense of humor, and smashing good looks. A few days later, Nico left again, when his manic surge returned.

Although I felt quite apprehensive, I eventually accepted Nico's invitation to visit him in Chicago, to meet his family. He and his teenaged daughter lived in a lovely, large, ranch-style home in an affluent suburb, surrounded by tall trees and a well cared-for garden, which provided Nico with his favorite relaxation activity. With his close-knit family living mostly within walking distance of one another, we both agreed we would have more privacy if I stayed in a hotel.

Although Nico had made it clear to his family that he and I had met as teenagers, and that I was married four years before he even met his own wife, I immediately regretted not listening to my inner voice, warning me to stay away from Chicago. Although his family treated me courteously, I felt Nico's deceased wife's ghost all around me. I could not help remembering my mother's warning, years ago, and was very conscious of everyone's eyes scrutinizing me, knowing full well they considered me an outsider and interloper, because I was not Greek.

After that, we met mostly in special hideaways, far from friends, relatives, and crowds, in small hotels and secluded cottages, to give us as much time alone together as possible. We were careful to keep the atmosphere around us calm and peaceful, quietly enjoying nature, taking naps and walks, listening to music, and reminiscing.

Nico loved to read to me, either poetry or passages from spiritual texts he used to quiet his mind. He also often brought along music tapes that played only piano accompaniment, for singers to practice with. He had a beautiful tenor voice and loved to sing operatic arias.

When I began to do research for *The Mezuzah in the Madonna's Foot*, he was my biggest booster, my most valued critic, and provided the kind of provocative suggestions that invariably drove me to a deeper, more personal exploration.

When a major crisis threatened to derail the book's publication, it was Nico's counsel that kept me hanging in and fighting for my rights.

With time, our lovemaking underwent a subtle transformation. From the initial wild, breathless coupling, it evolved into something akin to a long, slow meditation, like a Tantric ritual, accelerating gradually, holding still, slowing down the build-up, then reactivating the energy, until we were both unable to contain the impending explosion. What we ended up creating was a gentle, totally fairytale-like relationship, uncontaminated by banal, everyday realities, undisturbed by interfering outsiders, going from weeks, even months of longing and ever-building anticipation, to magical reconnections that grew in intensity and depth with every encounter.

Although I sometimes wished we could have had a normal life, living together, how could any ordinary, day-to-day, earthbound connection compete with our extraordinary relationship? Both of us had experienced the ups and downs of long marriages, raised children, and lived lives that demanded putting the needs of our families first, and often failed. Now it was our turn. We both knew we could never, actually, live together, without disrupting much of what we had built separately, without spoiling what was so special about our arrangement.

Nico was able to keep his commitments to his elderly mother and daughter, enjoy the rest of his growing family without having to endure the pain of their subtle disapproval of our relationship, tend to his garden, teach a Sunday school class and sing in his church choir, give seminars on restaurant management, and still make time to spice up and nurture our special kind of long-distance romance. Our arrangement made it possible for me to live my own life fully, maintain a close relationship with my family, nurture my connections with my long-standing circle of friends, and have the luxury of uncluttered time to develop as a writer and travel—without missing years of enjoying the excitement of an ongoing, intermittent, but always deepening love affair.

14

SEARCHING for My ROOTS

By 1988, I realized that if I was ever to reconnect to my true identity, I had to do it soon. Certain that my best chance of finding my Jewish heritage was where I first lived as a hidden Jew, like a modern-day *Marrana*, I decided to return to Spain. I had no idea how to proceed. I decided to consult the Los Angeles-based Spanish Consul General, to ask for his help and advice. I told him only part of the truth: that I wanted to explore the rumors about Spain's heroic role in sheltering thousands of Jewish refugees during World War II, when most democratic nations refused to allow them entry. I hoped it might motivate him to assist me, because, if the rumor proved true, it would enhance Spain's reputation, badly damaged during Franco's thirty-six-year-long Fascist dictatorship.

It worked. The consul knew that what happened in Spain was the best-kept secret of World War II, and he was excited, hoping that I might write an article to shed light on that paradoxical miracle. Between the two of us, we were able to contact and convince eighteen people in Madrid and Barcelona to speak to me: Jewish refugees who had fled to and remained in Spain, rescuers who had helped them, historians and diplomats as well as Catholic clergy and ordinary Spaniards who had been involved with providing a safe haven for the persecuted.

Worried about how I would be able to finance my venture with my limited savings, I tried to find some way to fund my research. When several Jewish foundations refused my requests for a grant, rejecting my project as too loosely conceived, and lacking in importance or interest, I decided to approach Spain's Iberia Airlines and ask if they might consider helping me. I told them the Spanish Consul General was excited at the prospect of finding someone finally willing to explore this long-ignored, mostly unknown part of Spain's history. That was enough of a recommendation to convince Iberia's regional manager, *Señor* Gabriel Perez, to offer me, as well as a companion of my choice, free flights to anywhere their airline flew, for the duration of my research! Although I warned him that I had no commitments from anybody to publish any of my findings, he did not withdraw his offer.

"This will be an important story. Someone will want to publish your research," he reassured me. The gift had no strings: all he asked in return was that I mention Iberia Airlines whenever my findings came out in print.

At that time, my journey was meant to be no more than a personal and private spiritual search, and making it into a book was not even a remote fantasy. But Iberia's generosity and *Señor* Perez' faith in me, as well as my own love for Spain, sparked in me a determination to make my research into something more organized, more historically relevant than I had originally intended, perhaps even making it publishable in some form.

After I returned from my first trip to Madrid and Barcelona, I showed a few pages of my research notes to my old friend, Bob Goldfarb. By then I had interviewed some of the refugees the consul and I had contacted. Like my own family, they had found a secure haven in Spain. But, unlike us, they had done so without first converting to Catholicism.

"You have the makings of a book here," Bob said and called a colleague in New York who happened to be one of the top literary agents.

"You must look at this material," he told him. "It's interesting stuff."

Without consulting me, Bob promised his friend I would send him the forty pages he had just read.

"Enclose a tentative proposal," Bob urged. "Give him an outline of what you imagine your book might end up to be."

"But I have no idea what it would become!" I protested.

"Don't worry about that, you can always change direction later. Right now all you need is an approximate projection."

Much as I appreciated Bob's enthusiasm and respected his opinion, I could not remember ever seriously considering the possibility that anything as concrete as a book would come from his efforts on my behalf. However, I found it unexpectedly engrossing to plot out some kind of direction plan for my research. As I wrote the outline, I actually began to visualize a real book emerging from the stories I collected and the historical events I planned to investigate. Not until much later did I come across a drawing from one of my art therapy classes, during graduate school, years ago. The assignment was to produce an invitation to a future event. What emerged was an ornately decorated invitation to a BOOK SIGNING!

Before I had time to consider how heavily a commitment to actually produce a book would weigh on me, the New York agent Bob had contacted put me under contract and began to approach publishers. On the basis of fewer than fifty pages and an outline, he soon produced a contract offering a $35,000 advance! This was especially surprising since I had, at first, received quick rejections from five major Jewish publishing houses. Each was unwilling to take a chance on someone with my lack of expertise, no discernible track record, and judged the diffused focus for the book too troublesome to take seriously. So when a major mainstream publisher made such an unexpectedly high offer, I asked my agent to explain how that miracle happened.

"A young, very inexperienced editor sent out one hundred requests to major agents, asking for Judaica. I sent him your proposal. I figured he was hungry, green behind the ears, had an empty desk, and thus time to read your stuff. He liked it and twisted his publisher's arm into taking it on."

When the contract arrived, I accepted the complicated details almost in a daze of disbelief, only vaguely aware of what I was signing, having never seen anything to which I could compare its terms. I simply went along with my agent's recommendations, trusting his expertise.

Although I hesitate to identify the publishers and other individuals involved in the ensuing events, the facts are true. Soon after the contract negotiations with my publisher were completed, all the papers signed, and the formal writing process had begun, I was informed that I was expected to provide a chapter outlining the history of the Jews in Spain as an introduction to my book.

"The average reader in America knows nothing about Spain and its history," I was told. "If your story is to make any sense to them, arouse their interest, we must first provide them with an historical and political overview to get their attention."

"I don't think that's a good idea," I argued. "Aside from the fact that I am not an historian, such a chapter would undermine the immediacy and cloud the intimacy of the personal interviews from which I plan to have Spain's history emerge organically."

"Trust me, we know our readers," the editor announced in a dismissive tone. "You may be the writer, but WE know best what will sustain the reader's involvement beyond the first few pages." She waited a moment to see if I changed my mind.

"Well, if you insist on refusing to provide the history chapter, we will have no choice but to hire another writer to do so."

Did I hear right?

"Hire another writer?" I asked. "Didn't I sign a contract that names me as the author?"

She did not bother to answer and continued: "...and give him $10,000 of your advance to do so."

I was outraged.

"Can they do that to me?" I asked my agent. "What about my contract?"

"You want your book to get published?" he asked. "If you don't want to write the foreword, let them hire someone else. What do you care?"

"What about my $10,000?"

"Once you sign a contract, they own you. To them you're a nobody. If you want to see your book in print, take the $25,000 that's left and consider yourself lucky!"

A week later, the publisher suggested I meet with a writer named Ira, an experienced Jewish author on the east coast. He had read my proposal and was enthusiastic about his assignment. I was flown to Boston and, despite my anger at the arrangement I was forced to accept, I found myself liking Ira. I trusted his assurances that he would consult with me frequently, and that he would make sure his work blended in seamlessly with my own. I returned home relieved, feeling that things might work out better than I first feared.

Shortly after our meeting, the publisher officially hired Ira to write the lead chapter, and my contract was amended accordingly. In addition to the agreed-upon $10,000 of my advance, he was also awarded a portion of my anticipated royalties. I did not think the arrangement was fair, but I was glad the troublesome issues had been laid to rest. What mattered was that my book would be published.

As I continued to write, I was instructed to send each chapter to Ira as soon as I completed it. I was puzzled by this request, especially because I was never given a reasonable explanation of how useful Ira might find any of it for his historical overview: the chapters I had sent him described my own childhood before we moved to Spain, my personal interactions with the people I interviewed, and how their stories influenced my perception of myself as a Jew.

Whenever I called Ira for an update, he reassured me: "You have nothing to be concerned about. Reading your chapters helps me shape my historical perspective." He added: "Remember, I am a professional writer, busy with other projects besides yours. So relax, we are on track."

Thus calmed, I kept on working, continuing to travel to interview people not only in Spain but Canada and several cities in the U.S. I forwarded each new chapter to Ira, hoping to hear from him, but most of the next two years passed without any relevant response or guidance from him or my editor. I tried to convince myself that "no news was good news," since, at least, no one was complaining about my work. Obviously, this is how getting published works, I assumed. Besides, I comforted myself, I have a contract to safeguard my rights.

During this time, one of my trips took me back to Madrid and then on to Israel, where I was scheduled to meet with renowned historian Haim Avni at the University of Jerusalem, as well as some refugees who had spent time in Spain during the war and eventually settled in Haifa.

By then, my research had informed me about Spain's King Juan Carlos' sweeping democratic reforms as soon he assumed the throne right after Generalissimo Franco died in 1975. I was impressed by his courageous stand against remnants of Franco's Fascist supporters who had attempted a coup in 1981 by invading the *Cortes*, Spain's parliamentary chamber, hoping to topple the monarchy and re-establish a dictatorship. They shot some of the ministers and threatened to take over the government if the king did not resign. Unlike his father, Don Juan, who fled into exile to Portugal years before, under political pressure, King Juan Carlos stood his ground; the insurgents finally surrendered, and the king earned the well-deserved reputation of a hero and has been revered by his people ever since. He is also greatly esteemed by Jews, who know that one of his first official acts as King was to attend a conference of Sephardic Jews in Brussels, where he asked the group to forgive Spain for past persecutions and promised they would be welcome if they wished to return to their ancestral home.

I decided that, since I was stopping overnight in Madrid before continuing on to Tel Aviv and again on my return, this might be a perfect opportunity to meet the king. I asked the Spanish Consul General to help me obtain an audience.

"And when do you expect to be in Madrid, *Señorita?*"

I gave him the dates of the two days I would be stopping in the capital.

"Do you think His Majesty might be able to see me on one of those days?" I asked.

The Consul informed me in a most officious tone: "His Majesty usually determines the time and date of an audience, not the visitor."

Although momentarily embarrassed by my *faux-pas*, I explained that I already had my airline reservations confirmed and numerous interviews scheduled in Israel.

"Unfortunately, those are the only two days I am able to be in Madrid."

While the consul agreed to send my request for an audience to the palace in Madrid, he warned me that my chances of getting approval were almost nil. Nevertheless, he asked me to provide him with three chapters of my manuscript, to make sure that what I was writing would not be an embarrassment to Spain or the royal family. As expected, by the time of my departure, I had not received an approval for my audience with the king. Ever the optimist, I left a phone number where I could be reached in Israel with the consular office, just in case.

Before I left, it occurred to me that, perhaps, someone from Madrid's Jewish community might have enough clout to arrange a meeting with King Juan Carlos. I made sure to be especially well prepared for such a momentous eventuality. I took along my best audio and video equipment, best camera, best dress, best jewelry, and packed those special items into a small duffel bag I planned to carry with me at all times, while sending everything else ahead as checked baggage. My companion/assistant and I were surprised that, unlike all the other flights provided by Iberia, we found ourselves assigned to first class on both legs of our trip to and from Madrid and Tel Aviv. "They must have run out of coach seats and bumped us up," I thought, delighted with the comfortable seats, elegant service and delicious food we were served.

As soon as we arrived in Madrid, I called my most influential contact in the Jewish community and asked if he knew anyone who could arrange a meeting with His Majesty.

"Lots of luck," he said. "Everyone wants to see the king, but very few succeed."

Next morning, on arrival at Madrid's Barracas Airport for our continuing flight to Tel Aviv, we checked our suitcases at the Iberia counter. While waiting for the attendant to issue our boarding passes, I placed my duffel bag on the floor between my feet. When I bent down to retrieve it, it was gone! My companion and I both looked around but saw no one with my bag. Panic-stricken at the thought that all my most important possessions might be lost, I immediately contacted the airport police.

"These thieves are very clever. They know that the real valuables are never sent through as baggage. Travelers keep them close. The crooks work in pairs: one jostles you, to divert your attention, or to upset your balance, then apologizes while the other one grabs the bag and gets lost in the crowd. It happens all the time, and we never catch them." My only consolation was that I did not have to meet the king: not only had I lost all my contact information and equipment, but now I would have nothing appropriate to wear for my meeting with the king!

Five days later, after I had interviewed Professor Avni and another historian at the University's Mt. Scopus campus, as well as several survivors who had escaped through Spain before emigrating to Israel, I found a note on royal-crested stationary in my mailbox. It was from the Spanish Consulate, notifying me that I had a fifteen-minute audience scheduled with the king at the Zarzuela Palace outside Madrid for NEXT afternoon—three days sooner than I was due to leave Israel!

Now I began to worry what I would wear for my royal audience! I rushed to Iberia's Tel Aviv office to exchange our tickets for the next available flight to Madrid.

The agent looked at the tickets and then at me.

"Who are you? Why do you have diplomatic tickets?" she asked.

"I don't know…I am just a writer. I am writing a book about Spain."

"Why should this entitle two of you to diplomatic tickets? Do you have any idea how much each ticket costs?"

"Probably about two thousand dollars," I guessed.

She laughed.

"Look. I'll print it out on the computer."

She showed me the printout.

"Fifty-five hundred dollars for each of us!" I gasped.

Then I remembered I had told the Iberia manager, weeks ago, that I was going to interview his king: I learned a long time ago that if you really want something to happen, you must act as though it is already a reality.

"Oh my God! It must be because I am going to meet with the king!"

The agent's attitude turned from suspicion to awe.

"OUR king? How lucky you are! He is a wonderful man. I envy you."

We left Tel Aviv late that night and arrived in Madrid early next morning. I immediately rushed to call my contact at the Jewish community to tell him I had obtained an audience with the king after all. He was delighted.

"Well, congratulations! Now you can ask His Majesty a question that those of us who live here have not dared to ask. After all, what can he do to YOU for asking," he laughed, "kick you out of Spain?"

"What do you want me to ask?"

"Tell the king there is a rumor going around that next year [1992] on the five hundredth anniversary of the Expulsion Decree, he will rescind it. Ask him if is true."

"Sure, no problem. I'll be glad to ask."

"Too bad you won't be able to meet the queen," he added. "She is the real *Macher* behind the throne, takes classes at our synagogue, and is friends with our chief rabbi. Besides, she is funny."

"Listen," I answered, "I am lucky to have a few minutes with the king. I'm not about to press my luck!"

We arrived at our hotel with less than an hour before I was due at the palace. I borrowed a white silk skirt and shirt from my companion, dressed quickly, and asked the *concierge* to hail a taxi.

"Al Palacio de la Zarzuela, muy rápido!, por favor."

The cabby turned around to look at me.

"La señorita va a ver al rey?" he asked with a sarcastic smirk on his face.

"Sí, voy a ver el rey. Soy periodista. Tengo muy poco tiempo." I showed him my invitation with its royal crest, indicating the time of my appointment in just ten minutes.

"Verdad? Ayyyy!!! Perdone señorita!...Pués sí, vamos muy rápido!"

With that, he took off on a wild zigzag jog in and out of traffic lanes, breaking every driving law while barely avoiding collision after collision, when a policeman on a motorcycle finally blocked his way. The cabby rolled down his window.

"La señorita es periodista. Tiene cita con su majestad el rey ahora mismo!" he yelled. *"Puede ayudarnos?"*

The cop looked inside the cab. When I showed him my invitation, he saluted me.

"Sigue me," he ordered and roared off, leading the way with siren going full blast, opening the congested traffic lanes like Moses parting the Red Sea, with our cab following in its wake!

When we arrived at the palace gates, we were already five minutes late. The motorcycle cop began to gesticulate agitatedly at the two sentries who were holding machine guns, standing next to their wooden guardhouses. One of them checked a list on a clipboard and asked to see my invitation.

"Pase, pase," he now said to the cab driver, waving us on. The motorcycle cop saluted, turned, and roared off towards town.

When it took another ten minutes to weave our way up through the lush royal gardens to the palace itself, I grew more and more concerned about being late. Once there, a man in livery opened the cab door and helped me climb out.

"Espere aquí para mi, por favor," I told the cabby, since I expected to be ready to return to my hotel in a very short time.

Inside, another uniformed servant escorted me up a lushly carpeted flight of stairs, motioned me to sit on a gilded chair in a magnificently furnished reception room, and asked me to wait. My heart was pounding as I looked up at a huge formal portrait of the king and queen hanging above a carved marble fireplace mantle, flanked by two flag poles flying the red and yellow striped Spanish state flag on one side and the crown-crested royal flag on the other. I thought about the beautiful gown and jewelry I had hoped to wear and felt embarrassed to meet the king so inappropriately dressed. A door opened, and an elegant, older gentleman appeared, bowed, and introduced himself as the minister of protocol.

"*Señorita* Alexy, I must inform you about certain palace rules," he said in heavily accented English. "Cameras are not allowed in the presence of His Royal Highness."

"No problem," I whispered. "My camera was stolen."

"...and neither are audiocassettes or video machines," he continued.

"No problem. They were stolen, too," I added under my breath.

Perhaps he will ask where they were stolen, I mused.

"What!" I fantasized him being outraged, saying. "Stolen! Here at our own Madrid airport! We must pay for all replacements!"

Of course, this never happened. In reality, the minister simply continued his instructions.

"His Majesty would also prefer that you refrain from taking notes while you are in his presence. He likes to speak extemporaneously and does not want to see someone scribbling away while he speaks. It interrupts the flow of the conversation."

"No problem," I mumbled again, certain it would be easy to remember ten minutes of conversation.

The minister now rose and bowed.

"Thank you, *señorita*. I now shall advise His Majesty that you are informed about our procedures."

"Sir," I said just as he turned to leave. "Does Her Majesty, the Queen, ever participate in such audiences as mine?"

"Yes, sometimes."

"Do you think she might be interested in joining us for this audience?"

"I shall ask her."

I could not believe I had actually dared to ask for more privileges than I had already been granted, but the minister seemed to see nothing unacceptable in my request and disappeared to consult his queen!

A few minutes later he reappeared, his face wreathed in a broad smile: "Her Majesty said she'd be delighted!" he announced triumphantly.

Now the double doors on the far end of the reception room swung open, multiple flashbulbs clicked away like so many castanets, the official royal photographers withdrew, and His Majesty, King Juan Carlos I, and Queen Sofía reached out to welcome me into another large room. As I entered, I could not help noticing dozens of intricately detailed, sterling silver replicas of all kinds of sailing vessels displayed among gold-embossed books on shelves in bookcases lining the walls of what seemed to be one of the royal libraries.

"As you can see, I have a passion for the sea," the king explained.

Tall and slim, quite handsome, despite a receding hairline, he was dressed in a light blue, short-sleeved shirt with red embroidered epaulettes and dark blue trousers. The left shirt pocket sported several rows of multicolored campaign ribbons; the right showed the embroidered blue wings and crown emblem of the Spanish Royal Navy Air Force. After shaking my hand, he bid me to sit in an armchair at a low, round table, facing him and his lovely queen. She wore a colorful, knee-length, silk print dress, matching shoes, and a strand of pearls.

Although I was prepared to conduct my interview in Spanish, the multilingual royal pair immediately put me at ease by addressing me in perfect English. Before I had the chance to utter my first question, Queen Sofía told me she had just finished reading the three chapters of my manuscript that my consul had sent her, and then began to ask me all about my own life! I was touched by her compassion for what she assumed was my "fear-filled, interrupted childhood," as she marveled how anyone could lead a normal life after such traumatic experiences.

I finally was given the chance to begin my own inquiry. Because I had been told that Spanish education was very parochial, and that public school curricula were still deeply influenced by the Catholic Church, I asked a rather delicate question:

"I am concerned that your children might grow up knowing very little about the history and contributions to their country's culture by Spanish Jews."

"But that is no longer true," the king said, and the queen quickly interrupted: "My goodness, you have been misinformed! Let me tell you about the many programs we have—seminars, contests, television series—all dealing with exactly what you mentioned, Jewish history, Jewish poets, philosophers, Jewish writers! Do you know there is a two-year waiting list for Hebrew classes at our major universities? Our people have a tremendous interest in Israel, admiration for what the Israeli people have accomplished under the most severe conditions. They have created a miracle!"

Now the king broke in: "The queen and I will be the first Spanish monarchs to set foot on Israeli soil when we visit Jerusalem next year [1992], for the Quincentennial Commemoration. We are greatly looking forward to it."

What a perfect moment for the question I was asked to pose!

"Your Majesty," I addressed the king. "There is a rumor in the Madrid Jewish community that, before that commemoration date, you plan to rescind the 1492 Expulsion Decree. Is there any truth to that?"

While the king prepared his answer, the queen quipped with a smile: "I bet Elie Wiesel told you to ask this question! My husband and I have met that wise gentleman on several occasions, you know, and it sounds just like him!"

By the time I acknowledged that I had never met the Nobel Peace Prize-winning author, the king was ready with his response to my question:

"I must assure you, had I been king at that time, I would never have permitted such a law to be passed in my country. However, it is now part of our history, and all we can do today is counteract its power, its intent, and its influence. As the queen just informed you, we are doing just that. Besides, our country's constitution mandates freedom of worship for all religions, and thus has automatically displaced the old decree."

The queen now asked if I would like to be introduced to Madrid's Chief Rabbi. "I know him well. He is a wonderful man."

"Thank you, Your Majesty. I have missed meeting the rabbi twice before and now will have to miss that pleasure again, since I am due to leave Madrid next morning."

I looked at my watch and was shocked to see I had been with the royal pair for over an hour!

"Your Majesties, please forgive my overstaying my visit. But before I leave, I have a great favor to ask."

I turned to the king and continued.

"I have been here much longer than I anticipated. So much has changed in your country since I lived here. Because I was not able to take notes, and I would not want to misquote you, may I ask you to write a few words to include in my book about how you see your own and your peoples' relationship with Jews today?"

"Tell me what you would like me to say, and I'll be glad to send it to you."

"No, I thank Your Majesty, but I would prefer the words to come from your own heart."

The audience was almost over. The queen asked me to send her a copy of my book as soon as it is published, and the king promised to send me his thoughts. We shook hands, the queen rang a bell, and a guard appeared to escort me out to where my trusty cabbie was waiting for me.

Next day I arrived back in Los Angeles, and three weeks later an envelope with a royal crest, addressed to me, was delivered to the Spanish consulate by diplomatic pouch:

> *In 1992 Spain commemorates Sefarad '92, an event which has very special connotations for the Spanish as well as the Jewish people, whose ancestors had to leave Spain in 1492, a land they loved and where their culture blossomed for so many centuries. This anniversary is a good occasion to consider the negative impact of prejudice and intolerance, prevailing in Europe*

during that time, and above all it is an occasion to pay tribute to the golden age of Spanish Jewry.

The poetry of Yehuda Halévy's, the scientific and philosophic innovations of Maimonides, and the profound contribution to astronomy of Abraham Zacuto, just to cite a few names, are inscribed with golden letters in the books of literature, philosophy and science. We should also remember the example of tolerance and peaceful coexistence given by Jewish, Christian and Islamic communities in Toledo, which made that city one of the most extraordinary centers of culture during the twelfth and thirteenth centuries.

This book also contributes to our common history with a very important and not very well-known chapter. By means of personal accounts we are told how the lives of many Jews were preserved during the Second World War, when thousands of foreign Jews were sheltered in Spain or granted asylum in Spanish embassies throughout the world. Although these episodes could be considered a historical paradox, considering the situation in Spain at that time, they are in fact not so surprising, because they originate in a profound historical connection.

The expulsion of Jews in 1492 did not sever the link between Spain and the Jewish world. Jewish culture was kept alive in Spain thanks to Crypto-Jewish families, and outside the boundaries of the peninsula, first in the Mediterranean basin and the Near East, and later in the Spanish territories of North and South America. While Spain was taking its language and culture to the New World, the dispersed Sephardim disseminated their culture to the far corners of the globe, for which the Spanish people should be thankful and proud.

I still remember, with great emotion, the warm welcome Queen Sofía and I received in 1987 at the Sephardic Temple in Los Angeles, which marked the official reencounter between the Spanish crown and some of our most beloved brothers and sisters. Since then, the Spanish and Jewish peoples have rediscovered the best side of our common past; my son, the Prince of Asturias, had the pleasure of awarding the Humanities Prize, which bears his own name, to the Sephardic Community.

Finally I want to give my warmest thanks to Trudi Alexy for her decisive contribution to a better understanding of our two communities, by writing a book that will certainly constitute a discovery in the year commemorating the discovery of the New World.

Signed: His Royal Highness, King Juan Carlos I

On October 17, 1991, King Juan Carlos I was awarded the Elie Wiesel Foundation's Humanitarian award. What follows is an excerpt from the address by Elie Wiesel during the award dinner:

> *As a Jew, I am committed to the memory of our history, the history of Israel and therefore its right to live and fulfill its destiny in security and peace.*
>
> *As a good Jew, I believe in the obligation to remember. We remember the good and the bad, the friends and the foes. We remember that during the darkest era of our recent history, Spain gave shelter to countless Jews who illegally entered their territory.*
>
> *And I remember that five hundred years ago, clinging to their faith, Jews were forced by your ancestors to leave Spain. Could they have imagined that their descendants would meet five centuries later in an atmosphere of tolerance, understanding and friendship? History does have imagination as well as memory. In 1950, when I visited your still-tormented country as a young correspondent for an Israeli paper, I had an eerie feeling I had been there before. Many places seemed familiar. I thought I "remembered" events, names, experiences...*
>
> *When I came to Toledo I thought I could hear—some 850 years after his death—Yehuda Halévy's powerful poem of nostalgic love for Jerusalem:" Libi ba-mizra'h ve'anokhi besof maarav": my heart, said he, is here in the East, but I am here, at the other end of the West...Barcelona evoked for me the great thinker Nahmanides. It was in that cathedral that he defeated Paolo Cristiani during their famous disputation. Granada? I knew the city from Shmuel Hanagid's war poems. Abraham Ibn Ezra was born in Córdoba....I have always been particularly fond of him. He was a fatalist, who believed he was meant to be poor, always. In one of his songs he wrote: "If I were to sell candles, the sun would never set, if I dealt in funeral shrouds, no one would ever die...As long as I lived."*
>
> *Oh, yes, Your Majesty, I think of Spain and I see the noble figures of Menahem ibn Saruk and Joseph ibn Abitur, of Shlomo ibn Abirol and Maimonides. How poor Jewish philosophy and poetry in general would be without their legacy.*
>
> *The history of your people, Your Majesty, and mine, have registered many moments of glory...Three religious communities lived and worked and dreamed together for many, many decades...*
>
> *But our past also contains moments of despair. When I think of the great luminaries of medieval Spain I cannot help but remember the Inquisition*

and its flames...the public humiliation of Jews who wanted to remain Jewish...The Expulsion and its endless procession of uprooted families in search of new havens.

Still, while no man is responsible for what his ancestors have done, he is responsible for what he does with that memory. What you, Your Majesty, have done with yours has moved us to honor you tonight.

We honor your convictions and your beliefs, your principles and ideals; we honor your commitment to humanity. Having witnessed the evil in fascism and dictatorship, you chose to bring democracy to your nation by restoring its taste for religious freedom, political pluralism, and social justice. Your personal courage in opposing the attempted coup d'état won you the admiration of free men and women the world over.

We applaud your wisdom in separating religion and state, your compassion...your sensitivity to and concern with Jewish fears and hopes...your emphasis on symbols...Your decision to visit a synagogue next March, on the five hundredth anniversary of the Expulsion Decree, offers proof that Spain, represented by Your Majesty, has overcome its past and faces the challenges of the future.

That is a noble gesture that will live in our collective Jewish memory forever.

Reading Eli Wiesel's words, confirming so many of my own research findings, I felt as though I had received the Jewish Good Housekeeping seal of approval.

15

GETTING PUBLISHED

As soon as I returned from Spain, I was determined to find out what was happening to my manuscript. By now I had grown quite worried and suspicious. However, I found myself breaking out into a cold sweat each time I reached for the phone to call Ira. Part of me clearly wanted to know the truth, but another part of me was terrified to hear it, whatever it might be.

As my anxiety grew, I had the following dream:

> *I have a beautiful two-year-old child. One day a famous promoter approaches me: "You have an amazingly talented child, she has all the qualities needed to become a star. You don't have the connections to make her into a star. I do. If you will sell her to me for $10,000, I will guarantee she will become famous."*
>
> *"I looked at him, laugh, and say: "You must be crazy! Sell you my child? Never!"*
>
> *The promoter continues: "You selfish woman! You call yourself a mother? You are depriving your child of the best opportunity to fulfill her potential! Shame on you! Your child will hate you when she finds out you denied her this once-in-a-lifetime chance!"*
>
> *I shudder with shame and agree to sell him my child.*
>
> *Later, the promoter contacts me again: "As wonderful as your child is, we have decided she needs a bit of work, you know, a little nip here, a tuck there."*
>
> *With that he shows me my child: an arm protrudes from her head, a foot from her belly,…*

I awoke screaming.

All along, I had been sharing my concerns with Nico, and he kept advising me to trust the process and all would turn out well. But when I told him the dream, he immediately knew what it meant and advised me to call Ira. "He needs to know your unconscious is picking up something that is not quite right. He must level with you."

I called Ira and told him my dream.

First there was silence, and then came a muffled sob.

"Ira, what is it?" I asked.

"They told me to take you out of each chapter," he confessed, almost inaudibly. "They just wanted an historical account, without anything personal, without any interaction between you and the people you interviewed."

I could not believe what he was saying. I had trusted this man!

"But you read my proposal, you called it MY spiritual journey. You agreed to work with me. How could you break your promise to me and do what they asked?"

"By the time they told me, I had no choice," he admitted, "because they had me under contract!"

I was stunned.

"So what have you done with my book? Now that I know what happened, can you send me what you wrote?"

"The editor has already approved the altered chapters, and although I was warned not to send you anything, I feel I owe you at least that much."

A few days later, I received Ira's manuscript. It had a twenty-five-page historical foreword, in a dry, straight-forward style, not at all the way I would have written it: no personal comments, no little stories to illustrate the effect on the victims created by Spain's medieval, draconian, anti-Jewish laws. The interviews were equally straightforward questions and answers, no sense of two people connecting emotionally and sharing memories of similar experiences. This was definitely not the book I had intended. But I felt that, if I ever wanted it to see the light of day, I had no choice but to accept the status quo. I was unwilling to jeopardize the book's publication. Just as my dream foreshadowed and forewarned, I was ready to sell my "child" for $10.000!

By this time, I had met Matthew, the Crypto-Jewish priest on whose personal research of his ancestors, as well as his own life experiences, the final "Secret Jews" chapter of my book was based. My contact with Matthew happened by accident, and his story turned out to be most compelling and revealed one surprise after another. He stressed that his medieval Marrano ancestors, practicing their ancient rituals in secret, were always afraid to be found out. To fool their persecutors, they buried a *mezuzah* in the foot of a clay Madonna by their front door and kissed it coming and going.

That story felt so symbolic of the *Marranos'* commitment to hold on to their Jewish traditions, despite constant danger, that I found myself deeply moved. I was determined to abandon the generic, dull title I had given my book and change it to *The Mezuzah in the Madonna's Foot.*

When I called my editor to request the change and told her the name I had chosen, her response was a gasp: "What a crazy title! Who in hell will know what you are talking about? No way!"

We argued for nearly a month, and I eventually convinced her to agree to the change. Shortly after this happened, the publisher's division to which my book had been assigned was shut down, my editor was fired, and I, along with approximately 145 others, suddenly became authors with legal contracts but no publisher to fulfill their terms. I was certain that this would be the end of my newly-named, "almost-book". For three months, all the aborted books floated in a free fall, with little hope of anyone ever seeing them in print.

Then Simon & Schuster came to the rescue and offered to adopt the orphaned authors. The following account came to me second-hand, but from a reliable source. Since the new publishers knew nothing about any of their new adoptees' books, they hired a young marketing *Wunderkind* and told him: "For God's sake, don't bother to read any of the books. Look at the cover blurbs, the reviews, and the titles, and tell us which books you think will be commercially successful."

He picked my book BECAUSE HE THOUGHT PEOPLE MIGHT THINK IT WAS ABOUT *MADONNA* (THE SINGER!!!)

As soon as I was assigned a new editor, she called me.

"I just read your proposal. What happened? Where are YOU in this manuscript? And what is this historical stuff at the beginning that sticks out like a sore thumb and does not even sound like you wrote it?"

"I didn't write it!"

"What do you mean, you didn't write it?"

Now I told her all about Ira, and what we had been forced to do.

"Well, we'll just have to send the manuscript back to Ira and ask him to put you back in!"

"Please, let me have it. I have my original text on my computer, and I want to make the corrections. If you don't approve, you can always send it back to Ira and let him do it. But I want first crack at it."

"But he has been paid to do a job, and it is unsatisfactory. He should make the changes."

"It's not his fault. He was told what to do. Just give me a chance first, please."

She sent me Ira's version, and I systematically proceeded to make all the changes: delete the history chapter and restore the deleted personal interchanges and comments between my interview subjects and myself. It took nearly two months, but, in the end, the book was back to how I had intended it to be.

When I sent it to the editor, she called:

"NOW WE HAVE A BOOK!"

Ira proved to be a gentleman about everything, although he refused to return my $10,000 advance.

"I did the work I was told to do, and you would not have been able to do it your way and get published. But I think you should remove my name from your "Acknowledgements." I should no longer be given credit for any part of the work. It is truly all your book now."

◆   ◆   ◆

It so happened that the very day I received the yellow galley advance copy of my book, I was invited by the Spanish Consul General to attend a reception for Spain's Minister of Culture, *Señor* Arias, whom I had met on one of my trips to Madrid. When I arrived at the Wilshire Plaza Hotel and joined the other guests, I realized that this was not a cocktail party for which I had gotten all dressed up, but a business meeting. Everyone else was in suits while I sparkled in sequins. An oval table had approximately twenty name cards next to yellow pads and pens.

The Consul General and Minister Arias sat at the head of the table. The other participants turned out to be professors of history, literature, visual arts, and theater, from various local institutions, who had participated in cultural exchange programs with their Spanish counterparts. As they took turns introducing themselves, I realized I was the only person there without at least one Ph.D. As each spoke in detail about his or her particular project, I kept wondering why I had been invited since I, alone, had no project to report on. I was second to the last person due to speak. When my turn came, I worried—what could I possibly say?

The instant I heard my name, I rose, apologized for not having a project to discuss, held up my yellow book galley and added, shyly: "But I wrote this about Spain. It is my first book and it has just been published by Simon and Schuster."

I sat down and could barely wait to run for the exit. As soon as the last guest next to me finished her talk, I rushed towards the door. But before I could get out, two male participants blocked my way.

"Miss Alexy," one gentleman began, while the other stood at a discreet distance. "I understand you are not affiliated with a university. Is that right?"

"Yes."

"And you do not have a doctorate, right?"

"Right."

"And you are not an historian, true?"

"True."

"And since this is your first book, you cannot really call yourself an author, would you agree?"

"I suppose so."

"Well, then, how in hell did you get Simon and Schuster to publish your book?"

I tried hard to hide a smile.

"It must be a miracle," I replied.

The second gentleman asked basically the same question.

I walked out, holding my head high, glad I wasn't an academic.

◆   ◆   ◆

Ira and I have met several times since my book was published, and we remain on good terms. *The Mezuzah in the Madonna's Foot* has been in print and selling in hard copy and paperback (by Harper San Francisco) for twelve years as of this date (April 2005). When its sequel, *The Marrano Legacy: A Contemporary Crypto-Jewish Priest Reveals Secrets of His Hidden Life*, was published by the University of New Mexico Press in 2003, and I went out to promote it, interest in *The Mezuzah* re-emerged stronger than ever.

16

TACKLING UNFINISHED BUSINESS

In 1993, a friend suggested I join her in attending a seminar called "Religion and Psychology" at a local college. She knew that both subjects had long interested me, although it had been some time since I had last read or taken any classes on anything psychological. My own psychology practice had dwindled to just a handful of patients because, for several years, my energy had flowed primarily towards my writing and involved a lot of travel for research. I had by then become a member of a Jewish congregation, and Judaism and my relationship to my Jewish identity remained a major part of my focus, so I agreed to sign up. Only when I sat down in the auditorium and read the brochure providing information about the subject and panel of experts participating in the seminar, did I see that Martin was one of the presenters! I had not seen him for eighteen years!

After my initial shock, I decided that this unexpected meeting would give me an opportunity to clear up a question that had been on my mind for nearly twenty years. I waited until the lunch break, told my friend I had business to take care of and walked up to Martin.

"Long time no see."

The look on his face was one of utter disbelief, as though he were facing a ghost.

"God, you look great," he whispered, blushing.

"Yea, I know," I replied, smiling. *The Mezuzah* had just been published; I looked better than I had in ages, and I knew and felt it.

"Want to have lunch, for old times' sake?" I asked. "I brought a sandwich."

"Oh...yeah...sure," he stammered but did not at all sound sure. We sat on the grass under a tree, figuring we would have privacy there because everyone else sat on chairs around umbrella tables. At first there was mostly small talk. When I

told him about Simon and Schuster publishing my book, he countered by bragging about his own books (all published by a tiny psychology-oriented company!). Then there was a pause, and I asked:

"Why did you tell my husband you had refunded to me all the money we paid
you for all the years of my therapy?"

As I watched his reaction, it was clear he was trying to figure out where my
question came from. What he did not know was that, years ago, when I was
about to complete my studies for my Masters' degree, I called my ex-husband to
remind him he still owed me four thousand dollars from our divorce settlement. I
had asked him for the money several times before, to no avail, and now I needed
it to finish paying my tuition. I finally asked my attorney to send him a formal
request. He in turn asked his attorney to send me a response, in which he advised
me to stop pressuring for the money because he had information *"that monies
paid on your behalf had been spent for other purposes."* I did not have a clue what he
was talking about, so I called him to ask for an explanation.

"Recently our friend Martin and I happened to be attending a wedding of
mutual friends," my ex-husband told me, "when he suddenly came up to me and
told me he had returned to you all the money we paid him for your sessions. This
came clear out of the blue. Then when you asked me for the money I supposedly
owed you, I figured you were lucky I did not sue you for whatever he refunded
you. How much was it, anyhow?"

I was nearly speechless. Martin! That lying bastard!

"Did he show you any proof that he had given me the money?"

"Are you implying what he said was not true?"

"Ask him for proof. He won't have any. What he claimed is not true."

Now, all these years later, I wanted to have an answer. I continued to confront
Martin.

"So, why did you lie to him about returning to me all the money we paid
you?"

"I did give you money" he insisted, visibly flustered…"What about the birthday money I gave you to put away, you remember, for our island in the Mediterranean, for when we…?"

"A total of four hundred and fifty dollars?" I sneered. "I spent it on books. So
why did you lie to him?"

Now Martin became agitated. He rose and stood over me, gesticulating wildly
as he hissed his words at me:

"He was spreading all kinds of dirty rumors about me...I could have lost my license! Maybe if he thought we were just having an affair..." He stammered: "Besides, YOU seduced me!"

I stared at him.

"My God, after all these years, you have learned nothing!!!"

He turned and bolted back into the auditorium.

I was seething. I thought about how I had struggled, with the help of four other therapists, to finally learn to believe that what happened to me was not my fault, to accept the fact that I had been especially vulnerable, and that Martin Temple had used his position of power to keep me tied to him in virtual bondage for fourteen years. And now, after all these years, he had the nerve to tell me I SEDUCED HIM!!! When I got home, I wrote him a long letter, recounting my memories of what had transpired between us during the years he controlled my psyche, and described what it took for me to get free and recover.

"The fact that you lied about refunding to me the money you were paid for my therapy is proof that you obviously knew that accepting payment for treatment while you had sex with me was doubly immoral, unethical, and illegal," I wrote. "So, since you professed to have refunded the money to me, I expect you to do just that, NOW!"

I added an approximation of the fees paid and therefore owed and sent off the letter by registered mail. A few days later, I got the following note:

Dear Trudi,

I cannot identify at all with the devil you portrayed in your letter. My judgment may have been off here and there, but you looked so wonderful when we last met, have become so successful, that, obviously whatever transpired between you and me, could not have been so harmful. I wish you continued success and good health.

That letter fuelled in me a rage of revenge. Now I was finally strong enough to fight back. I spent several days on the Internet looking for an attorney willing to take on a test case of "therapist sexual abuse" that happened so long ago that its statute of limitations had expired. The attorney I found was willing to accept my case pro bono. He was excited when he heard my story and was eager to proceed. He was particularly pleased that I had boxes of letters and poems to prove my claims. He had successfully participated in helping to extend the statute of limitation in cases of "child sexual abuse" and saw very little difference between the two: as in incest, the therapist in effect takes on the role of parent or even God, giving him unfair, even unlimited power over his patient. The resulting problems often lasted a lifetime.

I called Martin and told him I intended to sue him. Then I sent him an official letter: "If you want to see your name all over TV and the tabloids, continue to hold onto your position of innocence. I need you to admit what you did was wrong. I don't want what you did to me to happen to someone else. You owe me restitution."

Within an hour of receiving my special delivery letter, Martin arranged a three-way conference call between himself, his attorney, and me. What he offered first was laughable, but we eventually settled on a satisfactory sum of money. It was not nearly the amount I should have gotten, but money was never the object.

I never went any further. I did not want to hurt Martin's family. I have disguised him sufficiently here to make it difficult for anyone beside himself to recognize him. In order to sue me for telling our story, he would first have to admit he is, in fact, Martin. I doubt he would want to risk that…the attorney I found is still eager to take him on, and the boxes of his letters are still in my safe.

I got what I really wanted: Martin's admission of responsibility and guilt. I used his check for publicity to promote *The Mezuzah in the Madonna's Foot.*

POSTSCRIPT
GOOD BYE, NICO,
GODSPEED!

As we grew older, a back injury made it hard for Nico to travel, so I offered to go to him, since, by then, much of his family had scattered, and I was able to spend more private time with him on his own turf. He had long practiced a weekly ritual of making a huge pot of delicious soup and bringing jars of it to many of his life-long neighbors. When I accompanied him on one of these rounds one Friday evening, he made a point of introducing me thus to his friends: "My wife was my second love. I'd like you to meet my first and last love." The final time I saw him, he drove me to the airport and we sat right in front of the flight information desk, waiting for my departure announcement. We were holding hands, deep in conversation, when I suddenly heard a "last call" for my plane.

"Why didn't you call me," I asked the attendant, annoyed. "I'm about to miss my flight!"

"Lady, I called you three times. You just didn't hear me!"

An embarrassed, rushed hug good-bye, and we were parted forever. Soon after that visit, one of Nico's sons called to tell me his father had died of a massive heart attack. "I know what a special place you had in his heart."

I was touched by his sensitivity and caring when he sent me copies of the loving testimonials given by Nico's children and grandchildren at his funeral. Sobbing, I reached for a bound booklet containing a collection of 365 quotations that Nico had sent me years ago. Those wise words had shaped his consciousness and brought him spiritual comfort throughout his life. They were the thoughts of philosophers, poets, artists, religious and political leaders, writers, and many others whose minds and hearts he admired. I had turned to his list of inspiring words again and again whenever I missed him most. Now that he was gone, that booklet became even more precious.

Here is the introduction to Nico's collection of quotes:

> *Thirty-eight years ago, my two-and-a-half-year-old son was killed. I was babysitting, engrossed in writing a letter and did not hear him slip out the back door behind him. He was crushed beneath the heavy wheels of a garbage man's truck.*
>
> *After an extended period of despondence, depression, and even attempted suicide, I sought professional help. One of the things suggested to me was that I should begin a collection of words that have particular significance for me.*
>
> *It was Sigmund Freud who said: "Words and magic were in the beginning one and the same thing, and even today, some words retain some of their magical power."*
>
> *It is my hope that some of the words that were magical to me might work their magic for you and contribute, somehow, to better health and recovery. (Signed:) Words of Magic from a Manic Depressive.*

He added:

> *To Trudi, with deepest appreciation for all you have meant to me, and to so many others. God bless you always.*
> *All my love, Nico.*

I turned once again to his booklet, after days of mourning my loss of the man I loved, and one of the quotations I happened to open to was an excerpt from Morris West's *The Shoes of the Fisherman.* I went to look for the quotation in my copy of West's book. Tucked between its pages were copies of my correspondence with West, one letter telling him about my scary call to Nico, after years of disconnection, hoping to prove our love for each other had not been an illusion. I also found one of my mother's letters, containing her reaction to West's book,

> *"He was alright, but I think you could do a better job writing the story of your own life…"*

Nico's reminder that words contain magic once again proved prophetic and healing. Those that inspired him will forever remain my personal gyroscope, helping to center me whenever I lose my balance. Not a day goes by that I do not thank God for twice bringing Nico into my life.

How could God still be withholding his forgiveness for my past transgressions when he has blessed me with Nico's love and so many other miracles?

Although ensuring God's continuing forgiveness remains a lifelong effort, I now know it must begin in my own heart, by facing myself honestly, taking responsibility for both good and bad choices, making amends whenever appropriate, and finally forgiving myself.

SOME of NICO'S 365 WORDS
of MAGIC

1) Memory is the one gift of love that cannot be taken away.

2) Life is the mystery. Faith is the magic.

3) Choice, not change, determines human destiny.

4) Doubt is another way of knowing.

5) Music is liquid architecture (Goethe)

6) Neurosis is buried suffering (E.M. Peck)

7) There are no strangers in the world, only friends we haven't met yet.

8) All of the beautiful sentiments in the world weigh less than one lovely action.

9) Happiness is beneficial to the body, but it is grief that ennobles the mind. (Proust)

10) Forgiveness is not so much the suspension of penalty, but the reestablishment of intimacy.

11) I have never met a man who is not my superior in some ways.

12) And of the happiest moments which were wrought within the web of my existence, some from Thee, dear heart, have their colors caught; There are some feelings time cannot benumb, nor torture shake, Or mine would now be cold and dumb. (Byron)

13) Most of our behavior is an attempt to feel valuable, and our days are spent proving we are someone, that we exist. (Tillich)

14) Lord, give me patience, and give it to me NOW! (Saint Augustine)

15) Do you have a problem? Take it to a child. You'll get your answer in the child's eye. (Marc Chagall)

16) The tragedy of life is not death, but what dies inside us while we live. (Norman Cousins)

17) Ruin hath taught me thus to ruminate: That time will come and take my love away. This thought is as death, which cannot choose But weep to have that which it fears to lose. (Shakespeare)

18) You can give without loving, but you cannot love without giving.

19) Man's capacity for justice makes democracy possible, but man's capacity for injustice makes democracy necessary. (Niebuhr)

20) In Hebrew, the word for "work" and "worship" are identical.

21) You would not seek me had you not already found me. (Pascal)

22) Some see things as they are and ask "why". I dream things that never were and ask "why not?". (JFK)

23) Experience enables you to recognize a mistake when you make it again. (F. P. Jones)

24) Children are afraid of the dark. Adults are afraid of the light.

25) We are not human beings having a spiritual experience. We are spiritual beings having a human experience. (Thailhard de Chardin)

26) He jests at scars that never felt a wound. (W. Shakespaere)

27) There is but one thing that cannot be taken away from us,—our attitude, and it is in the realm of attitude that we can shape our salvation. (V. Frankl, *Man's Search For Meaning)*

28) Nothing of the heart is ever lost: it lives on in other hearts.

29) Prayer is when we are talking to God. Meditation is when we are listening.

30) We are never satisfied with the present; we only use the present to arrange the future. We so neglect the present that it and the past only serve as means to some unsure future. And so we never live, but only hope to live; and as we are always preparing to be happy, it is inevitable that we should never actually be happy. (Pascal: *Pensees*)

31) Yesterday I met a whole person. It is a rare experience, but always an illuminating and ennobling one. It costs so much to be a full human being that few of us have the enlightenment, or the courage, to pay the price...One has to abandon altogether the search for security, and reach out to the risks of living with both arms. One has to embrace the world like a lover, and yet demand no easy return of love. One has to accept pain as a condition of existence. One has to court doubt and darkness as the cost of knowing. One needs a will stubborn in conflict, but open always to the total acceptance of every consequence of living and dying. (Morris West, *The Shoes Of The Fisherman*)

Author's parents' wedding photo

Author at six months with mother

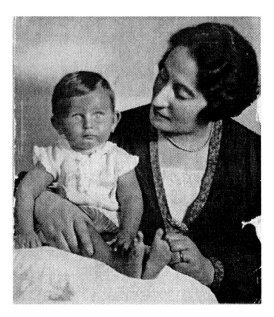

Author at six months with grandmother

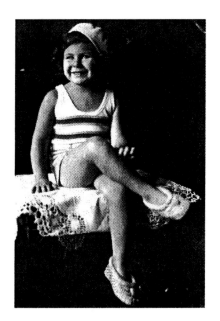

Author's "Shirley Temple" photo, 1932

Author and brother in 1933

Family passport photo, 1938

Nico in 1944 the day he and Author met

Author's photo sent to Nico in 1975

Nico and Author in 1980

Author and Abdellatif in 1964

Saki Karavas in 1975

Author with King and Queen of Spain in 1991

About the Author

Alexy lives in Los Angeles, surrounded by a large family. As a much requested member of the United Jewish Communities Speakers Bureau, she lectures widely in the US and Canada.

978-0-595-36054-3
0-595-36054-8

Printed in the United States
36890LVS00005B/379-429

9 780595 360543